ADVANCE

"The Loveseed exists within each of us. Our work in this lifetime is to uncover it and allow it to direct us. Kathleen Hanagan offers a road map that shows us how to do this, and is a priceless gift for the world."

~ Patricia Fero LMSW, author of *What Happens When Women Wake Up?* and *Sacred Marching Orders.*

"I love this book! A wise and eloquent message from the heart of higher intelligence. *Live* it and transform the world."

~ Bill Pfeiffer author of *Wild Earth, Wild Soul*

"Written with elegance and extraordinary vision, *Loveseed* is a compelling call to action told through masterful storytelling. Indeed, given the tumultuous state of the world we live in, Kathleen Hanagan's message to choose love is needed now more than ever."

~ Heidi DuPree, RN, CTN
award-winning author of *Awaken Your Greater Health*

"Kathleen Hanagan's heart opens on every page of *Loveseed.* Her book nudges you to go deep into your own soul to get in touch with your essential truth. You take an inward journey with Kathleen to learn the territory of the heart, as well as adventures with shamans in far away places. to This book may be perfect for healers or psychotherapists who are committed to helping others heal through the power of love and align with a bright future. As she says, 'The future can heal the past.'"

~ Kaya Singer, Author of *Wiser and Wilder, A Soulful Path for Visionary Women Entrepreneurs.*

"Kathleen Hanagan's book, *Loveseed*, has the power to create a personal shift, a deep awakening, for its readers. Eloquently written, it is penned from the very 'loveseed' she is describing through personal experience, exercises, prayer, and wisdom. It reaches past the intellect and goes directly to the heart. Every word is imbued with transformational potential that true authenticity reveals. This is a book to savor and allow its well-earned wisdom to activate the loveseed within you."

~ Asandra, author of *Contact Your Spirit Guides*, Schiffer Publishing Ltd.

"Occasionally someone comes along and offers an opportunity to change what needs changing. With *Loveseed: The Template For Birthing A New World*, Kathleen Hanagan comes bearing such a gift. In a soul-crushing world screaming for more depth, meaning, and connection, Kathleen's gift has the power to reveal what breaks our heart and returns us to the path of our inspired, highest purpose."

~ Dr. Gary Stamper, *author of Awakening the New Masculine: The Path of the Integral Warrior*

LOVESEED

THE TEMPLATE FOR BIRTHING A NEW WORLD

By Kathleen Hanagan

Wilmington, DE

Author Contact: KathleenHanagan.com

Thomas Noble Books

Wilmington, DE

www.thomasnoblebooks.com

Library of Congress Control Number: 2018959127

ISBN: 978-1-945586-14-9

First Printing: 2018

Editing by Charlon Bobo, ArmedWithInk.com

Internal Design by Balaji Selvadurai

This publication is designed to provide accurate and authoritative information regarding the subject matter covered. It is sold with the understanding that the author is not engaged in rendering professional services. If legal, accounting, medical, psychological, or any other expert assistance is required, the services of a competent professional person should be sought. Client names have been changed to protect identities.

Table of Contents

Dedication

Long before this book was written, the reason was written in my heart, which was formed in the fiery battles between my passionate father and me, and in the unwavering care from my loving mother. Both of you, Peg and Henry Hanagan, have blessed me with more reasons to be grateful than you will ever know, including the wounds I have healed and transformed into gifts. I dedicate this book to you.

Three people, like no others, have opened the door to my heart so much that I must share it with the world. To my children Antje, Katrina, and Jonathan, I also dedicate this book to you. Thank you for showing me how *loveseeds* grow by blossoming before my eyes.

Preface

I write the preface to this book with great humility. Though I finished the manuscript ten months ago, many events transpired that brought progress to a dead halt.

One of them was the collective catastrophe of a national election wrought with mud-slinging and lies. I felt paralyzed for several months. The other was a personal earthquake that rumbled through my life until I gained enough perspective to return to my message.

Naturally, in writing a book where personal memoir and a call to awakening are paired, a willingness to evolve radically is required. Experience itself is a great teacher, and the further integration into a practical personal cosmology takes time, reflection, and humility.

I had invoked that willingness and felt triumphant when I completed the manuscript. I knew that it was far too long and that I needed to edit and polish, but that it carried the message I longed to share with the world. I gave the book to a few trusted friends and my amazing mother, who was 86 at the time. I had written a great deal about my family and devoted a key section on *dharma* to my mother's story. I had included the struggles with my father in the book, as well as the gifts I received from him from that very struggle.

Since one of the main messages in my book is a clarion call to wake up and question what we call "authority," I found myself up against the unspoken agreement to never expose or shame my family. It was certainly not my intention to do so, and yet my story has deep roots in my family.

The conversation with my mother was exquisitely painful. She loved the book and said that it was very beautiful and that she was proud of me... and she was very disturbed by the story I told of an event that happened between my father and me when I was four years old. She also understood that I was making a key point by sharing it but could not believe that it really happened the way I remembered. She said if she had known, she would have done something about it. She said she would not have stayed with my father if she had known that he would do such a thing. She did not believe my father capable of what I recalled.

I was stunned. I felt her pain. I felt mine. She felt mine and she felt her own. I didn't know what to say other than that it was what I remembered. I just felt so much pain in that moment.

Being a woman of deep faith, my mother prayed for a sign to know. On the way to church that very day, she turned on the radio and there was a show on *false memory syndrome*, which according to Wikipedia, "describes a condition in which a person's identity and relationships are affected by memories that are factually incorrect but that they strongly believe."

What are the chances? She doesn't usually turn on the radio. She heard what she had prayed to hear, which is that we often remember the past with distortion and confabulate a story—this is my addition—especially when the past is traumatizing. She asked me if I had possibly recalled that my father threatened to hang me out the window, rather than that he actually did.

As a psychotherapist, I knew in that moment that it made no real difference to me or to what subsequently unfolded in my life whether my father actually did it or not. He spoke it. He threatened to do it. I recall him fumbling with the screen with his elbow while he held me with both hands. I recall the deafening sound of fear going off in my head like deadly bombs, my lips quivering, and becoming angry and tough after that.

As a daughter, I realized how important that distinction was to my mother. In that moment, I accepted it as "truth" that my father was so angry he threatened to drop me out the window, but that he did not actually hang me out. In fact, I don't think he ever even raised the screen. I don't really remember. I was too busy dissociating from my fear in order to survive. That was the point of the story for me, which I had lived with for more than 60 years—the fact that it scared me so much that I dissociated from the feelings of that moment. But for my mother, that story rocked her world. And I had assumed that she had known.

No need to argue that she had known and had suppressed it. That was not the point. This was not a courtroom. This was my life, my relationship with my mother, and the book I had written. It was about the story of my life. I needed enough love to let go of my old story to include both my four-year-old self and my mother.

My mother realized how what had happened had affected me and the subsequent anger and struggle between my father and me that colored the life of the entire family. She knew how much he loved me and how challenged he was by me for never being willing to back down when he was unfair, often to my own detriment. Because of him, I had swallowed my fear and now fearlessly questioned his authority, over and over.

The conversation ended with love, each of us honoring the other's feelings. There wasn't really more to discuss, as is so often the case in life, where we will never know the "objective truth." Somehow, there needed to be room for both of our experiences moving forward, and I needed time for that integration to happen inside me.

Subsequent studies in a form of sound healing have taught me that, energetically, our parents are on either side of our solar plexus, about ten inches away from the body, in the biomagnetic field that surrounds us. They are always there, informing us how much of our personal power it is safe to own and express. Imagine that! We are all captive to their potent influence until we return to the essence of who we are beyond the stories we have about them. As a psychotherapist, I have witnessed over and over that children in the very same family describe the same parent in totally different ways. The middle son describes his mother as warm and present, while the oldest daughter describes her as cold and indifferent. There are many reasons for this, from the subjective nature of the child, to the circumstances of the parent at different times, to the inter-subjective nature of the relationship. If the mother had a strained relationship with her own mother and the daughter has a personality like the grandmother, or if the mother projects that onto her daughter, a very unique situation is created.

Where does that leave any of us? We become who we are and how we are due to multidimensional and multigenerational forces that are apparently beyond our control.

That is what this book is about—the journey to know who we truly are in our deepest essence—our *loveseed*—that transcends all our stories.

It is true, as Byron Katie says, that without our stories, we are pure love.

Kathleen Hanagan

To support readers in deepening and embodying the teachings of the book, there is an exercise for each chapter that can be used as spiritual practices, which can be found at the following link: https://www.kathleenhanagan.com/loveseed-a-new-world/

On this page, you will also find deeply moving guided meditations by Kathleen, including a Loveseed meditation to connect you to the sweet spot of eternal aliveness within you.

Acknowledgments

A deep and abiding thank you to my father, Henry Hanagan, who told me when I was a young girl that he knew I would write a book one day. Thank you for that seed you planted dad!

Thank you to friends Sherry Cupac and Rose Levenberg, who believed in me when I did not, and to friend Dava Money, who served as muse and mirror throughout the creative process. Thank you to Patry and Sara, sisters of the heart and soul. You have held me strong.

Thank you to David Hazard, whose guidance helped me know I could write what was in my heart, and to Peggy Leckie, who knew just when help was needed. Thank you to priestess sister, Sherri McLendon, who kept me accountable to my big vision.

Thank you to all the GoFundMe donors who believed I had something of value to say, and Laurie Senders, whose steady presence has been a gift.

Thank you to Pat Fero, who knew when I needed a reboot, and to editor Charlon Bobo, who stepped in to seamlessly co-create and raise the frequency to match the vision.

Thank you to Lynne Klippel for reminding me to remain true to my inner feminine knowing, as I birth this book into the world.

And last but certainly not least, a heartfelt thank you to all the many clients I've worked with over the years. You have taught me not only that transformation is possible, but also that it is a mystical magical process, that compassion is its fuel, and that it is our birthright as spiritual beings on this misty blue planet of the possible.

CHAPTER 1

Take a Chance on Love

Saving the World

In my dream last night it was all so easy:
With this gizmo in my hand,
light as a feather, softly gleaming.

I could vacuum trouble and sorrow there.
I could siphon anger from a terrorist
(restoring him to father, brother, son)
and from fury the gizmo could distill
an elixir to banish cancer from every child.

Governments can't make peace,
but the gizmo could. Armies can't bring
back laughter from the lost, but the gizmo did.
The patent for this simple Stradivarius stood
enshrined above the Constitution. It replaced
the car, the prison, money, and war.
Some called it canto, ballade,
Almeh, lieder, poehma. Lullaby.

Everyone had one free.

– Kim Stafford

Imagine... just imagine that you have the power to create such a world, in which everyone had one of the gizmos. Not alone, mind you, but with others who believe in the possible, and on the razor's edge of evolving awareness— people into cocreation. It would be a world like the one John Lennon sang about in *Imagine* in 1971, when I was 19 and going through deep spiritual transformation so typical of that age: nothing to kill or die for, no religion, and people living in peace.

I had friends fighting in Vietnam at that time, while I had the privilege of being a freshman at a top East Coast college. It was during this time that I became aware of a seed that was planted in me long before. Some would call it a *godseed*—a *starseed* from another galaxy—one that was programmed to sprout in unison with millions of other *starseed* children. I call it a *loveseed*. Some say John Lennon's *soul* purpose when he wrote the lyrics to *Imagine* was to activate those seeds, and he lived nine years more to make sure they were watered.

Did I lose you with that one? *Loveseed?* Stay with me and let me take you into my world and into the souls of people I have encountered and counseled. I've been a psychotherapist for 30 years, and I have watched a lot of seeds sprout. When it happens, it is beyond beautiful, and I have had the highest honor of helping countless tender plants grow into sturdy trees.

There is powerful and wise Ursula, who came to me in deep depression, unhappy with her nursing career and grieving over not being able to have a child. Part of her healing was to embrace that she herself is a natural and potent healer, which her depression guided her to. Not only did she end up giving birth to a healthy boy, she birthed her *loveseed* into existence and continues to help others as an energy healer and naturopath. I served as a spiritual midwife, and today I am still in awe of the organicity of the unfoldment, when there is a safe place to be fully seen.

My three children have been my greatest teachers in learning this skill and have made it clear to me that a person's *loveseed* is entirely their own. You can attempt to project, overlay or infuse your personal agenda, but *loveseeds* only thrive when they are deeply seen and accepted *as they are*. Whether nurturing our own *loveseeds* or the *loveseeds* of others, deep seeing and acceptance are the sunlight and water of the soul.

Not everyone I have had the opportunity to help has thrived as much as Ursula. Some people don't feel worthy of joy, believing they must atone for sins that aren't even their own. Others refuse to let go of their pain and suffering and dash hope against the rocks. Their weary lives take the shape of that pain.

I recall Patrick, a big, tall Irishman with a tender heart. His childhood was entirely devoid of warmth; a kind of emotional winter. Patrick was a hottempered and intensely-feeling man and had repressed his true nature throughout his life, until a point several years into his marriage. He was hardwired to marry a "cool" woman, Jean, who was the perfect one to trigger the pain that caused Patrick to bury his *loveseed* as a child. Jean loved Pat, but her natural style felt to Patrick as if she was always raining on his parade. Twenty-six years earlier, Jean said something so wounding to Patrick that he made a decision never to be happy again as long as she was still "that" way. He was Catholic and would never divorce, so he felt stuck at a very deep level.

When I met them, they had been married 32 years and had raised five children. They were miserable and had even tried a hand at helping other couples in trouble. They were good at that, which made them even more confused as to why they made no progress with each other. As a seasoned couple's therapist at the time, I tried everything I knew. With all that I understood about the forgiveness process, I continually found myself back at square one with Patrick, who remained unwilling to budge in his decision. It was as if he had taken a vow of unhappiness, which he was willing to endure in martyrlike fashion.

As Patrick hid his *loveseed* from Jean, he also hid it from himself. He was unhappy as an accountant, and wanted to be a lawyer, but he claimed he was too depressed from his untenable marriage to do anything about it. As far as Patrick was concerned, Jean had destroyed all hope in him.

Jean improved immensely, adopting a much less critical and scolding style, and there were many moments when I saw the light from Patrick's *loveseed* begin to shine. But there was always Patrick's perception, and Jean would inevitably say or do something that Patrick construed as the "same cruel behavior" and darkness again descended upon their relationship.

Patrick's sensitivity, intelligence, and desire to help others was all part of his *loveseed*, but he sabotaged work promotions that could have allowed him to use those gifts and instead remained stuck in deadend projects that left him feeling unappreciated. Patrick had made a second career out of being hurt by others at work, at home, and even in relationship to God, whom he felt had abandoned him like everyone else.

After as much improvement as was possible under my watch—including a consultation with a Jesuit priest who left the Church to get married—Patrick came away even more hopeless. He was struck that this priest had the courage to pursue his happiness, but he refused to allow that same treasure for himself. It would go up against the deep conditioning that sucked the joy out of his very life, and Patrick was loyal to that story. In fact, his conversation with the priest made things worse.

When I asked him what he thought could possibly help him surrender this painful stance, he looked at me with his big blue Irish eyes tearing up and said, "Kathleen, nothing and no one will change my mind. I will stay on this cold street corner forever. I know it. There isn't anything you haven't done that could help. There isn't anything more you could do. I have been too hurt to open up again. I'm sorry. I'm sorry about everything."

My mistake was that in that moment I believed Patrick. I accepted his argument for his own limitation, rather than believing he had a gizmo that "could vacuum trouble and sorrow." I colluded with his fierce resistance and failed to maintain a sliver of hope for this troubled man. I told Patrick and Jean that I would no longer work with them, and I gave up the dream of the possible for Patrick, when holding that dream is what he needed me to do the most.

Not being able to help Patrick is one of those regrets that sits in the Chamber of Wisdom within me—a sacred place where regrets have turned to wisdom. I now know that a person can never be so hurt that it's impossible to open up again. I know that behind the barriers to love is the deepest longing, contained in the infinite potential of a person's *loveseed*.

I hope you are beginning to understand the nature of these *loveseeds*. They are Source energy in a person's life, and they affect everything. Maybe some of you have recognized yourselves in Ursula, and you believe that the challenges you have now are there to make you stronger and more determined to bring forth your own *loveseed*. You have taken one workshop after another to raise your consciousness, worked hard in therapy to heal deep wounds, and in countless ways, tried to be the change you want to see in the world. You get so frustrated when you slide back into old patterns and allow yourself to get distracted from your burning desire to be different and make a difference.

You don't know what to count on, though. There is so much suffering in the world, and it breaks your heart. You end up feeling guilty for not doing more, and you want to find that sweet spot between your needs and the needs of others.

How do you become that person?

I celebrate you for wanting to find *that* spot. That sweet spot is found in the mature *loveseed* and can move you to do remarkable acts of kindness and generosity without getting burnt out. You arrive at that dynamic balance of meeting your own needs and the needs of others by fulfilling your vow over and over again to be your full self, with compassion. This develops the muscle of discernment. As soon as you are out of compassion with yourself, you are not able to be there for others, and it is time to turn your attention to yourself.

The desire to make a difference in the world is such a beautiful and powerful impulse that arises from the *loveseed*. When it is awakened fully, you begin to experience the *global heart*, which is the felt sense that we are all made of the very same substance, moving through time on this green planet. In mystical terms this is called Unity Consciousness, where all illusion of separateness falls away, and you experience a connection at the Source, or *loveseed*, with all other beings. A prerequisite is to care for your own heart first. Later we will address that ache in your global heart and what you can do to raise the vibration to a place of power. These sacred impulses must be nurtured if they are to bear fruit.

I am also speaking to those of you who are not at all sure why you are reading a book about *loveseeds*. You have no plan to save the world, and you may even have an aversion to mystical experiences of being in love with everyone. You are not really interested in raising your vibration to a place of power. You don't really get all this wounding stuff. While you admit that you have been let down so many times by the hope of love and think it might have something to do with your childhood, you don't want to spend time going back to what you tried so hard to escape.

You have learned to be ultrapragmatic, and you are a proud member of the "it is what it is" club. Besides, your parents may be really nice people now, or just moving on makes the most sense to you. Maybe you just don't know what else to believe, other than what you were taught, but it's not working for you the way it did for the people who taught you. You even wonder if it worked for them.

You long for more passion and sense of purpose in your life. It feels as if something is missing, and you thought maybe you could get a handle on it by reading this book. Besides, you don't want to be part of the problem.

There may even be some of you who identify with Patrick. You cannot accept what is, and you have no real hope, but you keep complaining because you secretly believe that there *is* something that can be done about your misery. When was the last time you complained about gravity? Let's face it, we only complain about things we sense something can be done about. Complaining is a form of resistance, and buried underneath the resistance is the energy of your *loveseed*.

If you are in this latter group, I want to tell you I fully understand your pain, your sense of defeated rage. They call it depression in the *Diagnostic and Statistical Manual of Mental Disorders*—the DSM. I call it despair.

I have been touched by so many of you over the years. I have been you as I have deeply-felt my own despair. I know why you have stopped believing. For you, all that talk about wounding is hogwash and just a fancy way of not taking responsibility. Life isn't easy, and you never expected it would be. You believe you need to watch your back, and sadly you don't trust anyone with your tender heart.

I mean it when I say that I have known despair. I really questioned the existence of everything. At one point, I was so far off-course, I nearly checked out. I became quite lost, eventually losing all my savings and worldly comforts. I lost my confidence, my vision for a future, and my health—most everything except one thing. During that terrible time, I had little energy for the world and drew inward to take sustenance from the essential kernel—the *loveseed*—at the center of my being. When you have nourished your *loveseed* over the years, as I had nurtured mine for so long, you come to know that there is a deep well to draw from during dry times. There is light in places you never imagined looking.

I wonder how I might work differently with Patrick now, many years later, after learning so much more about the conditions under which a person's *loveseed* begins to grow. Among the many things that Patrick taught me is that withholding your *loveseed* brings great misery, not only to yourself, but to others close to you. Indeed, two of his daughters did not want to come home much, given the tension between their parents, and the youngest had a hard time leaving home for fear of what would happen to them if she did.

Another key lesson I learned from Patrick is that if your *loveseed is* to grow to maturity, you must make a decision—a sacred decision—or what I call a vow. This sets the compass of your soul in the direction that will allow your *loveseed* to be fully expressed. As all the challenges (and there are many) arise to the full expression of your *loveseed*, this vow continually brings you back to your own "true north," which is essential for navigating the winding road of your own destiny, a word taken from *destinare*, which means "of the stars." Unless you know where you are going, the tendency to drift and go around in circles will persist in your life. You will notice the same old arguments, patterns, addictions, and of course, the same outcomes you have experienced for a long time. The *loveseed* hidden in the soul of each of us is made of stardust, and lights our way. **For each of us, the most important task is to grow that loveseed and shine forth its natural light to illumine the darkness.**

Maybe I **could** help Patrick now, for I have learned something more about fear since working with this couple more than 15 years ago. I knew a good deal about fear when I worked with them as a skilled clinician, but it is what I have learned personally as I have had to face many of my own worst fears that would allow me infinite patience with the likes of Patrick.

As Steven Pressfield says in *The War of Art*, "Resistance is experienced as fear; the degree of fear equates to the strength of Resistance." He added, "Rule of thumb: The more important a call or action is to our soul's evolution, the more Resistance we will feel toward pursuing it." He also said, "Resistance is always lying and always full of shit." Experience tells me this is truth.

Behind Patrick's enormous resistance was his fierce love. Had I listened to the music behind the words rather than the actual words, I would have heard Patrick's *loveseed* crying out for me not to believe this stubborn Irishman.

The real meaning of enlightenment

I have spoken a great deal about *loveseeds*, but you may wonder what the point is. It is not a plea to save the planet. The planet is just fine. It is humanity that struggles with the multiple levels of chaos and change happening all at once. We, with our limbic systems that require rhythm and connection, our soft bellies, and our tender hearts, cry out for what is real. Humankind is quickly becoming desensitized and adapting to the great deficit in nurturance that afflicts us all.

Many are afraid of what is happening, and predictions of humanity's end abound, including the fear of artificial intelligence becoming more powerful than human beings. Maybe the thought of humanity's end is disturbing to you and you prefer to believe that love will win out; that the light will overcome the darkness. I still prefer to believe that as well, just as I would hope against hope that if someone I love had an illness, there would be something that could be done, while at the same time I would be fully cognizant of the odds and implications.

I would hold out for a miracle to the end, so before you continue with this book, you may as well know that about me. The *Course in Miracles* defines a miracle as a *shift in perception*. This book is about miracles and will open you to them.

The future is in potential form, and we each have a say in how things turn out. This book will help you understand the depth and breadth of the power you possess and will show you ways to become masterful as you create a future where truth will have a renewed meaning. Outmoded beliefs will shift and transform into conscious paradigms that allow you to embody your own co-creational nature.

This is the definition of enlightenment: the process of elevating our consciousness to let in the light of higher awareness to the point that we embody and live it. For this to happen, a person must answer the call to step onto a path of conscious awakening toward personal mastery. This book is to guide you on that path, and I am your companion guide, as well as an elder. According to Michael Meade in *The Genius Myth*, "An elder is someone who has extracted wisdom from the struggles of their own life." I will share with you how I have done that, so you can benefit from what I have learned, and extract the wisdom from it as you discover your own way of knowing.

This book affirms the infinite capacity for transformation we all have, all the time. It offers a path of healing the divisions inside each of us so we can do our part in healing the great divisions in the world today. It seeks to offer a more universal language for the ultimate mystery of human life—a language whose origin is in the heart of each and every one of us. This book shows you the way to the wellspring of legitimate power and greatness inside you and requires both humility and discipline to perceive.

We come with the memory of the Source we evolved from, and rather than a far-off place, hell is what it feels like to be in alignment with the absence of Source. And yes, we must all pay for liberation. There is always an exchange of energy, a ransom of sorts, which is the journey of our lives. The price is that we must take the journey consciously. We must face our fears, and as we do, we reclaim and integrate our lives at a higher level.

Every fear is a fear of the self inside, and your challenges are what you need to reclaim yourself as Creator. You cannot be the light and hold another person or situation in fear. Facing your fears changes everything! You eventually come to see them as allies.

As you read this book

Wherever you are coming from outwardly, and whatever your perspective on humankind, I imagine you desire to connect more deeply to what truly matters to you, and it may be that very longing that drew you to this book. It is also why I am writing this book—out of my own deep longing to express the *loveseed* within me.

This book is full of teaching stories, and knowledge in the areas of science, spirituality, psychology, mysticism, shamanism, and mythology which are meant to fill in gaps in your understanding and weave a larger cloth containing intricacies you can appreciate. Woven throughout the book are stories of several of my clients (names and details have been changed), the story of my own quest for enlightenment, and the wisdom I have gained from the highs and lows of that beautiful and difficult journey.

The book's progression is from understanding to experience to embodying a new template that transforms your actions. We are meaning-making beings who have a need to understand, as well as to enact. The exercises found at kathleenhanagan.com/birthing-a-new-world are meant to help you upgrade your felt experience of yourself and life and to activate a new multidimensional awareness in you—a genuine appreciation for the breadth and depth of the significance of your own life, no matter how little or how much you believe it matters.

Some of you will find the knowledge most useful, and others the stories, while others may appreciate the online exercises. I have intentionally woven the wisdom of many different disciplines together, as human beings learn differently and have diverse interests. I have also learned, from 30 years of working with thousands of people, that when a person both understands something and then embodies that knowing through feeling, a new kind of intelligence emerges.

Though there is plenty of information within the pages of this book, it is not a book about information. You can find all the information you could possibly want in a Google heartbeat. But information and even knowledge divide things into categories and certainty, and if that is what people really needed, there would not be so much suffering on the planet.

We are multidimensional beings, and you will begin to see with new eyes how many different dimensions come together to create the vibration of you and how much that vibration matters as you climb the mountain of your life with consciously-placed steps. This isn't a race. Remember to stop and gaze out for a moment and look at the horizon of your life and where you want to be. Look back to see how far you have come, even if you are just beginning. Look within to know where you are in this moment. Let this book provide a map, a template, that gently guides you on the way. You must widen your gaze and adopt a mindset of reverence to fully appreciate the deeper messages in this book, which are meant to open your Soul's vision.

Think of this book as my gift to you. The key is to allow yourself to receive the gift by softening around your mind and tapping into a curiosity and a deservedness. We all have shields of protection around our minds and hearts based on the past. Allow yourself to soften like a prayer, at the boundaries, and allow more fluidity of thinking and feeling. In this way your intelligence is taken to a place of grace, where you can receive a transmission of love.

Make love your only prayer

Each of you has a *loveseed* inside that longs to be watered. It is the seed of your own greatness, and it is made of light, which is actually love. It is connected to your challenges, gifts, and learning. It grows and becomes resplendent when you provide it with the proper nutrients and trim away everything that is not you. That is a big task, and it involves unlearning many things you have taken for granted. Though it is not easy in the sense of a quick fix, learning to be a master of love—maturing your *loveseed*—is worth every moment and every bit of effort you invest in it.

Your ego doesn't know this, though. The ego doesn't get anything out of enlightenment. We are trained to serve our egos, and it is hurting us—all of us. Growing your *loveseed* is not valued as much as growing your bank account or buff body. Each of us must have the courage to value it more because it is the intelligence that will save humanity. It is the lullaby we have been waiting for.

I want to tell you that you are up to it. Whatever has attracted you to pick up this book, I ask that you suspend your doubt for now and trust that the impulse came from your *loveseed*. The stories and teachings in this book will provide the nourishment, and your innate longing to be truly happy will provide the water.

This book is to help you move out of the trance where you are identified with your pain and your "issues." Trying to fix yourself keeps you in the illusion and triggers resistance. It assumes that something is broken. When we resist, we keep the illusion in place.

It does not take years of psychotherapy to learn a new way of being. Even if you are predisposed to depression, you have a lot going for you. When it comes to being happy, 50 percent has to do with genetics and was set from the moment you were born. But what if you got the short end of the genetic joystick? Are you doomed to a life of misery and depression? Not at all. The good news is that 10 percent of your happiness quota has to do with your environment, and 40 percent has to do with your attitude, which means there is plenty you can do to raise your happiness set point.

What is needed now is wisdom and uncommon knowledge that arises out of the darkness. This wisdom points to the hidden unities contained within the darkness *and* the light; the doubt *and* the knowing. It is the wisdom born of dancing with the mystery of life, loss, and rebirth, which we all share.

If you seek inspiration to stay the course, this book will shore you up and remind you of the vastness of your mission and of the power you carry inside you for a greater good. If you are adrift and have lost your way, this book will help you reset your inner compass toward your highest purpose and energize you once again to take the necessary risks you have been avoiding.

Knowing where you want to go is really important, so give yourself the time in reading this book to reflect on what gets stirred up in you. There is a river of joy within you, and you must attune to its flow. When you do this, you begin to know what is real.

If you are bitter, angry, and despairing about the world or about yourself personally, wondering whether you will ever live a happy and authentic life, this book will guide you to the peace "which passeth all understanding" according to Philippians 4:7.

To each of you who takes the journey of this book with me, I promise you that many ideas will come together for you. You will begin to tap into a higher intelligence and attune to its purpose in your life. The awakening effects of ancient mystical practices will come alive for you as I distill their deeper meaning and show you the way to your own power. When there is no tension between your transcendent being and your embodied being, you are free.

You will find a new code for your life—a template with a center that is synchronized with the evolutionary impulse our planet needs at this time. You will learn to resonate with the vibration of love in your deep heart. You will find yourself having greater courage and compassion, joy, and gratitude, and this will inevitably manifest in your outer life in the form of having even more for which to be grateful.

You can begin now. Take a chance on love. You have nothing to lose but the cage you created with your fear. Love is the strongest force on the planet, and you are its very source. And besides, if humanity is to truly thrive, it will be because enough of us are connected to our *loveseeds* to have it really matter.

Take a chance on love. Make love your only prayer.

CHAPTER 2

Where Is My Loveseed Hiding?

"We have the choice of two identities: the external mask which seems to be real... and the hidden, inner person who seems to us to be nothing, but who can give himself eternally to the truth in whom he subsists."
— Thomas Merton

We know it's the real thing

So why, you might be asking, do we get disconnected? Why does this awesome *loveseed* get buried so that people have to hunt it down like a hidden treasure? Maybe that is the point... that the ache of losing the connection is so powerful we try almost anything to feel it again. We are given a burning, inner pole star as a guide in the darkness.

The problem is, of course, we look in all the wrong places: drugs, sex, and rock n' roll. How many times have we settled for a pale simulation of the bliss of being connected to our *loveseed*? Worse yet is when a person falls into despair and believes it is too late.

Let's face it. Over and over, most of us have been willing to replace the connection to our *loveseed* or essence with all sorts of substitutes; a magic bullet that we can take with our bulletproof morning coffee, or a dazzling relationship that takes us off course and becomes another excuse for not living our purpose, with addictions and illusions of security that turn out to be sand castles of despair.

Yet, we hold out for the sweetness; for the love from the seed. We somehow know it's the real thing, indigenous to us, and not a derivative of our tribe of society. It is our very own star.

How is it that we all know when it is missing, are not sure how to find it, and long for it so deeply, while all the while it is *who we are* at our core? If it is our essence, our natural state, then why does it seem so elusive and inaccessible? And when we connect with it, why do we so easily let it slip from our grasp?

Seeing with new eyes

When you realize by seeing with new eyes that everything you think is "out there" is really a reflection of you, life takes on a new wonder. You are no longer separate from all that is. Einstein spoke about this "optical delusion of consciousness" as a prison, saying that "our task must be to free ourselves from this prison by widening our circle of compassion to embrace all living creatures and the whole of nature in its beauty."

There are a few reasons for this optical delusion of consciousness. Though the East and West have different ways of describing how human beings become "separated," the mystical branch of all religions shows a return to Source as the movement of a lifetime. It is often said that the longest and most challenging journey is from the head to the heart. In western psychological terms, we would say the person is well integrated.

The aliveness I connected to in myself arose after I let go of all concepts and, in fact, had become "empty of self." I passed through despair, deep grief, and anger, and at the very core of me was love. I had made this passage many times throughout my life, but this time I did it consciously.

I had tried everything, even a trip to India, but I found nothing to hold on to and finally let go of everything I had previously believed. I emptied myself, and since there were no ideas or rules to hang on, I came to rest inside the center of my being—my *loveseed*. This was the same movement away from separation and toward union and the same soft landing I had experienced over and over in my life, but this time, I was seeing it all with new eyes.

I have made my life's work a laboratory to help people come back to their *loveseed*. Each time I felt myself "separated," I learned more about how to come back, and thus had more to teach, from a deeply experiential level. I would synthesize this with knowledge from Ancient Wisdom sources, modern science of the brain and emotions, as well as the deep pool of human pathos that I dealt with day to day. Yet nothing has taught me like the Earth herself.

When I was a child, I would often leave the chaos of living in a large family to go alone into the woods, where I communed with plants and stones. My mother would pack me a lunch and off I charged, with walking stick and bandana. Nature had always been a source of sustenance, yet I had become a civilized woman who travelled to faraway places for enlightenment. I reconnected to that innocence at long last.

How could this be? No theory explains it all. Human beings are complex beyond belief, and yet so basic when it comes to their true needs.

The pivotal discovery of the unconscious

It is useful to go back to a time when the field of psychology was newly-emergent. Freud had discovered the unconscious, and radical new understandings of human beings and their development were being discovered by great and curious minds. Carl Jung was one of Freud's most prominent students, and eventually broke with Freud over basic differences in how each viewed the psyche. There are more than 400 documented references to pathology in the writings of Freud, and yet nothing devoted to healthy functioning.

Jung, on the other hand, was teleologically-oriented and focused on what is right or whole within us. *Teleological* comes from the Greek *teleos* and refers to a philosophical interpretation of nature and natural phenomena as possessing purpose or design. Everything is seen as purposeful in the service of self-actualization and healing. That includes symptoms, which Jung believed had meaning and are here to communicate what we need for our transformation to a higher order.

In Jung's view, depression, anxiety, and even psychosis are purposeful, and the role of the healer is to activate the transformation toward wholeness. The healer does not heal but guides the person to tap into his or her innate wholeness, or the *loveseed* inside. I concur with Jung, and I continue to experience awe as clients make shifts that are utterly courageous and from a far higher ground than the aggressive instincts that Freud believed to be the main drive of human beings.

We are also deeply indebted to Freud for discovering and identifying the existence of the unconscious or unseen aspects of human nature. He believed that the first five years of life are key formative years that create lifelong patterns, and he discovered and named the defense mechanisms of the ego. He believed that the die is cast young, and his work did not venture into the realm of Spirit where unseen forces can assist a person in making remarkable, and at times, radical transformations.

Jung, on the other hand, drew a more expansive and hopeful picture of a personal unconscious; a familial unconscious where beliefs and psychic patterns are passed down; a cultural unconscious that holds our tribal and religious heritages, as well as the collective unconscious—a storehouse of the universal archetypal patterns from the archives of humanity that each and every one of us carries. The word archetype means "original," and archetypes are our original templates or blueprints.

Jung believed that this innate drive toward our own wholeness is an inherited universal drive; part of the basic template of humanity. He called this drive *individuation,* which is a developmental process over time in which an individual moves further away from the divided and civilized self and closer to the true and undivided Self. In order to do this, we must own and release all that is not who we are. Before any wholeness can be found, we must each experience our brokenness, which leads us to our depths so that we may find the hidden unity in all things.

To Jung, the great enemy of mankind was normalcy— the attempt to fit in by contorting who you really are, thus creating a *persona* that is not you, and that you then present to the world as you. The danger is that you are lulled to sleep with this false sense of self, and you fail to realize it is not you. This is a state of being in which your personal drive for wholeness is rendered dormant, which for Jung was the only real "sin." I call it the *Trance.*

Burying the loveseed

When we are born, the vast love that we are comes in the form of a little helpless baby, with an undeveloped awareness. By being born into a small body, we are separated from the experience of pure love that we are. There is the experience of *embodiment shock,* the first major moment of trauma that is both physical and spiritual, leading to a felt experience of separation. Water births and other methods of softening this entry are used worldwide. If the birth is not too traumatic, the child remains connected to Source for some time. For all, we have literally passed through a portal into another dimension. We are left seeking a mirror to remember who we are.

Since we came from love, love is the only true mirror of who we are. As an infant, the first mirrors we encounter are Mom and Dad. Depending on how well Mom and Dad reflected back to us the love that we are, we may have begun burying our *loveseed* very early in life. Since Mom and Dad have also been searching for their *loveseeds*– usually not very consciously–they can only reflect from their limited sense of love, which is the legacy from their parents. With their help, we create a template that leads us to unconsciously seek similar mirrors in our close relationships. This is the cause of many of our relationship addictions and struggles and the great disappointment we inevitably experience when we expect to fill our emptiness through someone else.

Studies with infants and their caretakers show that sufficient positive affective interactions are needed for a baby to thrive cognitively, emotionally, socially, and even physically. These interactions are mostly mirroring or empathic responsiveness of mothers to their infant's expressions. It is as if mother and child are mirroring their loveseeds in this exquisite exchange. It is similar to falling in love when it happens and elicits many of the same physiological responses. All of this creates new neural pathways of connection in the child and the mother, literally rewiring their brains. The gift inside each person, their *loveseed*, is inexhaustible, yet it needs to be seen to be reflected.

Dysfunctional parent-infant interactions lack behaviors that encourage this sustained inter-subjective exchange. The healthy parent remembers to mirror her child, no matter what. Insufficient mirroring can leave a child lost and not trusting their own knowing, and can lead to a feeling of not being important or significant. Mirroring that is conditional on the child being or acting a certain way leads to a more rigid personality, and the feeling of never being good enough, no matter how hard the person works.

When the parent carries an unhealed wound and is not aware of the effect of the past, there is often a projection of unfinished emotional business onto the child, burdening the child with pain that it cannot metabolize and the child's *loveseed* begins to go underground. It has been proven that infants of depressed mothers are less responsive to faces and voices, among other deficits.

Studies have shown that both mothers and fathers spend less time mirroring male infants than female infants, and more time being physical with their male infants than attuned emotionally. In other words, males are less likely to have their *loveseeds* nurtured than females. The implications of that are not lost to anyone who sees what is going on in the world today. From one senseless mass murder after another, to the increasing number of terrorist activities worldwide, we see the results of males being separated from their *loveseeds*.

I once had a wise psychodrama trainer, Dale Buchanan, who said, "We are all living in a huge hall of mirrors, and it is a miracle when we are really seen, or when we fully see another human being." We are each wired to project, deflect, and protect, which leaves us incapable of clearly seeing another person.

Indeed, narcissism is the wound of the times. What this means is that countless people are not being seen, heard, and understood for who they are in their essence. The results are seen everywhere in the rise of hate crimes, addiction, and mental illness. The mother, disconnected from her own *loveseed*, from lack of support, familial wounds, financial strain, depression, or working two jobs, falls into a chair and looks into the light-filled eyes of her innocent infant. Rather than tap into the love inside her being and allow it to pour forth into the child, she feels empty, exhausted, and emotionally needy. The child, still sourced from love, looks at her adoringly, love pouring out of its eyes.

This can be a truly awakening moment for a mother if she can allow the love of the child to activate her own *loveseed*, which is able to resonate with, and take in, the essence of the child. This could elicit the pouring forth of love to the child. But if that mother's *loveseed* is so buried, this exchange will not take place and the infant becomes the mirror to the mother. This moment begins a process of dissociation, which repeats the myth of separation, over and over. The child has no mirror for who she is, and energetically begins to hide.

Dissociation—the poor man's detachment

How could something so seemingly innocuous as not responding to an infant have such a devastating effect? It is not actually the moment being experienced that is so devastating, but the fact that it keeps repeating itself throughout a person's life until they re-associate to the feelings that arose at that moment. This is the work of a lifetime, and it is essential to understand that such moments have happened all through your life. In particular, the woundings you experienced before the age of seven are etched in your emotional "hard drive," or unconscious. Your personality or ego formed around the wounds you experienced, causing you to dissociate and assemble the *you* that was safe to show. The more of you that is hidden, the greater the fear you experienced.

It certainly is true that the ability to detach from an issue or a disempowered way of seeing something is a skill everyone needs to have. The Buddha declared that all suffering comes from our attachment to things having to be other than they are. When we detach via transcendence, we move closer to our Divine nature. When we dissociate, we remain in a prison of misperception.

The truth is that everyone dissociates far more than they imagine. There are parts of us split off from other parts, and in many cases, all cut off from the *loveseed*. We all get our hearts broken early in life, either in the family, church, school, or with other children. We are not seen, heard, or understood by someone we have looked to for a mirror, and often someone else's fear or hurt was projected onto us. We were not deeply cherished as manifestations of the Divine, but often used to fill the unmet emotional and sexual needs of our parents and others. The moment of the perceived separation is so painful and/or terrifying that the human organism immediately dissociates from the felt experience, whether the pain is physical, psychological, or spiritual. To survive we naturally split off from the pain and identified with the parts that got us what we wanted and kept us safe.

Few human beings are entirely immune to the powerful influence of family and culture. Everyone adapts. I remember the day my son Jonathan dropped my hand when he saw his friends walking toward us. He was about seven and had already internalized the message that "big boys" don't hold their mother's hand.

As we adapted, we brilliantly began to develop a shell around our *loveseed*. Jung called this the *persona*, often called a "false self" or what Pia Mellody refers to as the "adapted self" in her book *Facing Codependence*. Most of us creatively adapted to an environment where it was clearly not safe to be fully who we were and we protected a place deep inside from getting hurt again. Our mantra became "no more broken heart." Because we couldn't selectively numb, we numbed the heart.

I once heard dissociation described as "poor man's detachment." It is an unhealthy and yet well-intentioned attempt to return to the natural state of detachment that is intrinsic to our being. We turn away or dissociate because it is instinctual. The part of your brain that perceives separation perceives death, since you cannot survive alone. This is the dilemma of being a multi-dimensional being in a body where we have limbic systems that attune us both to connection and to danger.

It has been found that many people who have endured tremendous trauma are highly attuned to the invisible world, as part of their dissociation is to detach to a place of comfort and light. They are often very sensitive, intuitive, and gifted in countless ways. After the battles with my father, I would hide in the closet and drift off in exhaustion and shame to a place of light, as I imagined my beautiful and strong guardian angel holding me. I became attuned to this world of invisible help and guidance.

Though we must not underestimate the power of our own woundings, we must not dwell there. We revisit consciously to heal and pluck the wisdom from the garden of experience and give our gift. **The gift we have to offer the world often emerges from the wound.** The neglected child becomes self-reliant and someone others can count on. The child whom a parent leans on and confides in becomes a very attuned therapist. A child who is abused physically grows up to run a shelter for abused animals, and on it goes. The Sufi master Pir Vilayat Inayat Khan says, "The same pain that can blemish our personality can act as a creative force, burnishing it into an object of delight."

We have not yet spoken of the outrageous and inhuman abuse that continues today. Some of you who are reading this now have been brutally abused, raped, criticized, rejected, humiliated, and disowned. I have been transformed by what I have come to know about the suffering of humanity. I, too, was hurt by a father who was disconnected from his *loveseed* some of the time and genuinely loving at others. It is confusing for children to have a parent who is safe and loving sometimes and not at others. **It makes you very vigilant and untrusting, and yet over and over again you will be tempted to put yourself in harm's way, because that is the template that was created**.

I recall studying attachment theory while earning my Masters degree in Social Work. There was a photo of a policewoman holding an 18-month-old girl in her arms, walking away from a woman with a cigarette her mouth. The baby was reaching over the policewoman's shoulder with both arms, screaming for her mother. The child had cigarette burns all over her arms and legs. That image is seared into my memory.

We know a great deal about trauma and PTSD now, thanks to studies with veterans. We know that neural pathways are formed during traumatic moments that can be easily fired later, if something similar occurs. Vets often have a hard time on the Fourth of July. Sound or scent from deep in the auditory or olfactory memory banks can trigger a massive panic attack. Yet that is true for all of us. We learned to dissociate far more than we know. You dissociate every time you go into a theatre, and often throughout the day, when you drift off, paying attention to the voices in your head, with full-fledged board meetings and family feuds, rather than be present with what is going on in your immediate environment.

Trauma induces very intense dissociation that can break through suddenly, causing a person to keep the original feeling alive. In the moment of being triggered, it is a huge challenge for a traumatized person to remain present in the moment. As trauma expert Kate Hudgins says in her book *Healing World Trauma With the Therapeutic Spiral*, "Introspection, the ability to look at one's self, the ability to take an objective stance, is impaired in trauma. There are too many unconscious pathological narratives."

Dissociation or detachment?

Each of us copes with trauma and emotional wounding in a unique way. What is devastating for one is not so for another. It is not so much the wounding that continues to hold us back, but the meaning we attribute to it that shapes our lives. Known for her books on parental child abuse including *The Drama of the Gifted Child*, Swiss psychologist Alice Miller says, "It is not the trauma itself that is the source of illness but the unconscious, repressed, hopeless despair over not being allowed to give expression to what one has suffered and the fact that one is not allowed to show and is unable to experience feelings of rage, anger, humiliation, despair, helplessness, and sadness."

It was Freud who first discovered the "repetition compulsion," which is a psychological phenomenon in which a person repeats a traumatic event or its circumstances over and over again. This includes reenacting the event or putting oneself in situations where the event is likely to happen again. By dissociating from the feelings of disempowerment (fear, sadness, anger, shame), you continuously attempt to gain control over them and unconsciously attract them into your life, ultimately for the purpose of reconciliation within.

If you had parents who were alcoholics or otherwise unpredictable, you may have become dissociated from your true feelings of terror and attempted to control the situation by being very quiet, helpful or otherwise invisible and under the radar so you could survive the storm of a parent's rage. The adapted child has grown up with those feelings inside, and along with those buried feelings is your buried *loveseed*.

When you dissociate from the body, you keep the Trance going, because the body remembers what the mind forgets. You disown parts of self, and those parts gets stored, for protection. Since we cannot destroy aspects of the self, there can be no transformation because the energy required for change is contained in the exiled parts. This dissociation is not true detachment, but rather resistance to the experience, as it is in the nature of the limbic system (ego) to resist things that cause pain.

True detachment can only come from your true nature. If you dissociate from your feelings by trying to "do" acceptance or detachment, you are striving from your ego and not from your true nature, or true self. It doesn't work, and the same old stuff comes up over and over until you re-associate within your own body/mind/soul.

Suppressive spiritual work where you "rise above" a situation without experiencing the feelings simply does not work to free human beings from the prison of the

Trance. In fact, it often backfires in the form of addiction, debilitating health issues, and other expressions of the disowned parts of self. When someone is very dissociated, ironically they become totally self-absorbed, because they are cut off from the experience they are actually having and remain entranced in their own fabricated reality. We have witnessed that in the shadow expression of many spiritual leaders who have been caught acting out their disowned inner sexual predator parts, while preaching celibacy.

You may have felt this with dissociated people. They have an impenetrable barrier that does not allow you to have much impact. You will not feel much nourishment from them, or trust them, as they are not fully present to what is happening and cannot offer you the gift of seeing who you are. On the other hand, when you are with a person who is detached from a place of love, rather than disassociated, you will feel a spaciousness in their presence and will often experience the precious gift of being seen. The ability to remain connected with your *loveseed* allows you to see the *loveseed* of another.

There is a saying in the field of recovery: "You must feel what you need to heal." It is true, and the ability to touch those feelings gently and release them has been explored every which way in the traditions of psychotherapy, energy healing, bodywork, meditation, and other healing modalities. In essence, I have learned that the way to heal trauma is to soften and bond with the inner child; with the *loveseed* within.

The emotional blind spot and the illusion of time

Why do human beings repeat certain behaviors and reactions over and over again, and then attribute the reason to something or someone outside of themselves—the boss, the partner, the lousy living condition? Even when it is obvious to someone else that the person has more ability to change things than they seem to believe, if the person is in an emotional blind spot, they simply cannot see where they possess the power to make a difference. They do not claim the agency they always have to create change because they do not feel their uncomfortable feelings fully, and instead project the cause outside of themselves, when the source is inside from another time and space—another Now.

These are moments when we say things like, "Why does this keep happening to me?" "Why do I always end up with unfair bosses?" "I have a way of attracting unstable women." We seem to "go blind" to what is happening in the moment if it is so frightening or shaming or shattering to what we believe about ourselves. At these moments, our brains are triggered to feel emotions that we dissociated from, because we have been afraid of what would happen to us if we felt them fully. This avoidance leaves the unconscious emotions within us, waiting to be felt fully in the present moment. **We create and attract these challenges due to the powerful vibratory point of attraction of our emotional blind spot, which is a match for the difficulty in our present life.**

Because they can really complicate our relationships and steal our joy over and over, what can we do about these blind spots?

Just as in driving, blind spots obstruct our clear vision. We project, disown, blame, and defend ourselves. We become victims of our own misperceptions and insist that someone or something else should change. We become triggered to drop into the reptilian brain, and we act out of the survival response: fight, flight, play dead, or submit.

Some of the answer to what we can do about blind spots is to understand the illusion of time that all humans buy into. Isaac Newton thought of time as a river flowing everywhere at the same rate, and Einstein evolved his view on time by unifying space and time into a single 4-D entity. Julian Barbour, British physicist and major proponent of the idea of timeless physics, has declared the solution to the problem of time in physics and cosmology as simply, "there's no such thing as time."

Barbour says that we are continually moving through a succession of Nows, and each configuration is an arrangement of all that is in the Universe. "Many different things coexisting at once. There are simply the Nows, nothing more, nothing less," says Barbour. There is no past and no future. The illusion of time passing comes from change. We observe changes and we decide that time has passed, when in truth, all the moments are happening now. Since some of the Nows are linked to others, there can be the illusion of the passing of time and a story of cause and effect, when in Barbour's reality, they all exist simultaneously.

The harsh words by your partner trigger the reaction of the child who was criticized by a parent. Losing a deal triggers the same feelings of being a failure you had as a child with ADD. The only evidence we have of a past is our memory, and yet memory arises from a stable network of neurons in your brain that exists now. Because linear time is an illusion, we are caught in the collective misperception of disconnection between causes and their effects.

One of the reasons it is so difficult to recognize that the chaos and pain of the present moment has its origin in the past, is because so much of what appears to be "time" has passed, and we fail to make the connection between how we are feeling in the moment and the past, because we don't stay with the feelings long enough to know.

Naturally, we can have here-and-now reactions to what is going on, if someone is harsh or unkind, which is quite different from when we are in our emotional blind spot. When it is here-and-now, we may feel hurt or angry, and we move on. But when we are in our blind spot, we have dissociated from our original pain, and the reaction to the pain of the moment is intense and at times debilitating, and all we want to do is make it go away. Our attention becomes transfixed by the person or event in the world around us, and we often feel the helplessness of the original pain.

If you keep moving too fast, the illusion of time does too, and you may succeed at keeping your emotional blind spots invisible in your rear-view mirror for quite a long time. Eventually however, your un-metabolized emotions will have their affect on your health, relationships, sense of purpose and sense of self.

Yet, identifying our blind spots is like chasing the wind. We cannot find the actual source, but we see the effects. To change the automatic reactions we experience from our blind spots is the work of a lifetime. It is the ability to create intentional positive change in our lives by unselecting reactions based on fear.

Recall my client Patrick. He was extremely fixated on the way his wife spoke and moved and breathed and how cold and critical she was. Patrick was running an endless loop tape of his experience with his mother that was triggered by the similarity in his wife, Jean. It is true that like most people, Patrick had chosen what is called an "imago match," which simply means that he married a woman who carries the "imago" or image that was similar enough to his mother to trigger his emotional body. Much of what he reacted to was his own projection, and there is a seed of truth in every projection. Yet even when Jean stopped being critical, Patrick continued to experience her the same way he did his mother. Jean could have no impact on Patrick, because he was caught in the *trance* of defending against more pain. He could receive neither the warmth nor the love he so needed.

Even if we repeatedly affirm and declare our desire for a loving mate, successful career, or financial freedom, if the emotional current in our subconscious is seeded with the vibration of unworthiness or self-doubt or poverty, we will indeed see that condition reflected in our outer world. **The Universe is diligent at reading the vibration of our emotions and delivering the people, circumstances, and situations back to us that match our energy.** It is an impersonal force that responds directly to what we put forth.

Romantic love relationships activate the energy of the *loveseed,* as each person is temporarily lifted to their best self by projecting their ideal onto the other and then expecting to be seen. As each person does this—with the assistance of phenethylamine, called the "love drug," a feel-good neurostransmitter that is released into the nervous system in the presence of the loved one—there is a period of "grace" during which the *loveseeds* receive plenty of water and sun, and each person gives freely. For many people, it is the first time they experience bliss.

There is a shelf life to this experience, however, as the brain's chemistry begins to adjust and acclimate to the other person. Unless each person undertakes the bold work of reconnecting to their own *loveseed,* a sense of "something missing" arises, the connection and passion wane, and conflict begins. The real reason one person leaves another is that they believe their *loveseed* cannot thrive inside the relationship, or they believe they must leave to find it. It's usually a combination of truth and projection that conspires to bring the relationship to an end.

Here are the three keys things to do if you want to be liberated from the tyranny of your emotional blind spots:

1. **Fully embrace the awareness that you have them.** Then you will look for them in yourself, rather than choosing the fool's errand of pointing them out in others.

2. **Ask for feedback from trusted people in your life and be willing to hear them.** You cannot see the nose on your own face, and asking someone you trust and love to reflect back to you something she or he believes you don't see about yourself, is so powerful. And sometimes it's positive! You may be dis-owning competencies or qualities that are awesome and beautiful.

3. **Take the time to feel your feelings fully.** Set aside time when something "grabs" you and breathe into the center of your chest to fully feel that powerful emotional center. It may also be in your belly, arms, or legs. Feel the feelings in the body, and breathe, with your mouth slightly open on the outbreath, so you allow the energy of the emotions to move out of you.

The breath carries the emotions through you and returns them transformed by your own awareness. You can name the emotions as well, but more importantly, feel them without judgment, and let them move through you, so you become free of their powerful effects. In this way, you avoid the old pain arising in the moment. You become a clearer channel for whatever is happening in the moment, responding with an unbiased mind and compassionate heart. You reclaim your role as co-creator with the free-flowing energy of the Universe.

Love is a wide-open doorway

Your loveseed secures your innocence for all eternity. You can always return to it, if you let go of what protects you. That means you must have the courage to revisit the original pain and heal your anguished heart. Those of you who have always felt a bit weird are ahead of the game. If you have felt as if you don't quite fit in, disenfranchised for whatever reason, and naturally go against the grain of the culture, consider yourself blessed. Weird comes from the Old English word, *wyrd,* which means "to follow a path of destiny." You are less likely to succumb to Jung's "nightmare of normalcy," which seduces you into thinking you have found your *loveseed* in outer acceptance.

I once met a woman who made a living as a psychic, and she called herself an "unwashed soul." In other words, her soul was not cleansed of the memories and knowledge from the realm of light, and she was acutely-attuned to the meaning and design of everything. She confided in me that her childhood was a torture chamber, and she had to become very empathic and psychic to survive. She saw the deeper reasons behind everything going on around her, and it nearly drove her crazy. A certain amount of amnesia has protected most of us "washed" souls from the too-muchness of life, until now. Not only do we no longer need this forgetfulness, but in fact, remembering will save us.

Some things you can forget about are perfection and the attempt to gain outer approval. You are already perfect and were never really wounded in the higher dimensions— that is, in your essence—despite what happened to your human self. Your attempt to get it right and all your "hustling for worthiness," as Brene Brown calls it, has taken you off-course. When you live with your loveseed buried, it is impossible to have high self-worth. According to expert Dr. Joe Rubino, "Studies show that at least 85% or more of the world's people suffer from some degree of lacking self-esteem." Self-esteem is the perception of one's self as lovable and capable. When you hide your *loveseed*, even if you don't know it consciously, it is hard to feel good about yourself.

You do not need years of psychotherapy to unlearn, shift and actually form new neural pathways, so that these old defensive tendencies can fall away. Love is a doorway—a huge, wide-open doorway—to step into a new level of consciousness and to make big change. There are as many expressions of love as there are snowflakes in winter. Every person who eventually wakes up, seeds the higher realms with their light, and together we co-create the planet of the possible, the template of which is imbedded in your *loveseed*. **The most radical thing you can possibly do is be fully yourself and allow the contents of your loveseed to come forth. No one else could possibly do what you are here to do.**

There have been many epic times in the history of our planet Earth. We have, however, never evolved at the rate we are now, technologically and in our ability to destroy. There has never been as great a need for us to collectively make the conscious shift to express our *loveseeds* as now.

On the personal level, it has taken all of eternity for you to arrive where you are now. There has never been a better time to awaken your *loveseed* and receive the precious gift.

CHAPTER 3

Receive the Precious Gift

"Since we cannot change reality,
let us change the eyes which see reality."
— Nikos Kazantzakis

The gift of the moment

As I began writing this chapter, the most wondrous thing happened that shifted the entire focus of what I was about to write.

Sitting on the deck of my friend's beautiful home on a mountain overlooking Jonathan Valley in North Carolina, I was reflecting on the conversation I'd had with my friend Nancy the day before about her painful breakup. I intended to write her something uplifting that could help her extract meaning from her sudden loss.

As I began writing to her, I heard a deafening sound and saw a hummingbird flying right toward me. It hovered six inches from my eyes and moved in a figure eight both sideways and back and forth.

The bird seemed to be speaking to me so fast and with so much information that my mind could not take it in. Fear shot through me, as its beak was inches from my eyes. The part of me that was not afraid was aware of the fear and of my heart pounding, and this part of me observing my fear realized the precious gift in the moment. A hummingbird, which I had previously declared my *totem* or "power" animal, was communicating with me directly.

The bird backed up as if responding to my fear, continuing to hover and communicate. My unafraid consciousness made a split-second decision to fully open my heart to the moment. I breathed big into my chest as if smiling with my heart. I was overcome with gratitude and awe. I could feel a moment of clutching, as if I wanted what was happening to last forever, and at the moment I noticed my ego getting attached, I surrendered needing anything more than what was. I immediately received a message that there is more than I could possibly imagine and that I can fully drink of the nectar of this and all moments. My body relaxed and I sat back expanding my energy field.

The bird flew to the far side of the deck, continuing the figure-eight movement, and my heart continued to open to what was happening. It returned to me, this time closer, and I felt the movement of air from the beating of its tiny wings. I breathed into my upper heart and felt a direct energy blast into the space between my eyes, or what is called the *third eye*. My heart was exploding out of my chest, this time not out of fear but out of gratitude, excitement, awe, and my own consciousness of what I was experiencing in the moment.

My entire body began to shake with an energy that was bigger than my personal energy, and I continued to open. I was even aware of having a wide smile on my face. We were breathing together. Our *loveseeds* were totally connected. A thought crossed my mind about the book. The continual hum of information that I was receiving at such a quickened rate slowed down so I could understand with my mind, and I heard the response: "Look at what you just wrote. It is the most important message." It seemed an eternity since I had written anything. I relaxed inside, yet my body was still shaking.

As my tiny friend backed up like a little flying saucer, I bowed in prayer and off it flew. I reached my arms up to him, sobbing with joy. I looked down at the page and the words, "Remember to fully receive the precious gift...." I was referring to the importance of receiving the precious gift from the relationship before cutting cords so she could experience deep body forgiveness for her friend and set them both free.

You may wonder at such an experience, and even write it off as a pretty cool occurrence that most people never have but is well within the realm of possibility. Yet for me, it meant so much more.

In 2006, while at a retreat in Malibu after returning from India, I had my first direct encounter with a hummingbird beyond the feeders in my garden. I was sitting on the side of a cliff overlooking the Pacific Ocean, in a deep dark pool of despair that was part of the disillusionment I had experienced while in India, and the shock of returning to the states after a year abroad. Everyone else merrily headed out to the green to practice the movement exercises that integrate and ground the teachings we had received. I simply could not join them and stayed behind, aware of my heart feeling like an inconsolable dying animal in my chest.

Out of what seemed like thin air, a hummingbird flew directly at the center of my chest, lightly touched it with its beak, and flew off. I woke up out of my dissociative lament in an instant, the doors to my heart flew open and a great sob released. I was back in my body and awake to the now.

Even though my body felt jolts of fear, what was different in this moment was that a part of me was not afraid. I had learned to consciously open my heart. This allowed me to receive the fullness of the gift of the moment. As a mirror to my consciousness, this hummingbird interaction was a reminder: it is up to me to either receive the gift of this moment or pass it by, writing it off as coincidence.

As within so without

We are co-creators with the rest of creation. We are an integral part of what actually happens in our lives all the time, even when it comes to hummingbirds and things that are seemingly out of our control. In other words, when powerful occurrences happen to you, they are far more than happenstance. Jung called this *synchronicity* – "temporally coincident occurrences of acausal events" – which holds that events are "meaningful coincidences" if they arise with no obvious causal relationship, yet seem to be related on the level of meaning. In other words, events that are connected by meaning need not have an explanation in terms of cause and effect.

For Jung, life was not a series of random events but rather the expression of the deeper order of things, which he and Pauli called the *Unus Mundus*, Latin for "one world." **This deeper order connecting what happens on the outside with that which is happening inside a person is a doorway to awakening.** Jung said that such experiences of synchronicity shared characteristics of an intervention of *grace*, often spoken about in religious writings where beings such as angels appear to humans in order to assist them in their Soul's quest for wholeness.

The Soul is the journey of attention throughout a lifetime. It is where we choose to put our focus, and the physical world around us is an exquisite metaphor for our inner beliefs and truths and perceptions of self. What you call reality in life is actually a relative reality created by your Soul in response to your current perceptions of self and beliefs. **Your Soul creates your external physical reality based on how you perceive your self in relationship to everything around you.** Hence, your Soul is your creator, your piece of God within, and you are ultimately the master of your own destiny as your Soul is constantly telling you what to create.

Just as your Soul based the creation of your early life circumstances and experiences on your initial perceptions of self and unresolved emotional material you brought to this world, it is now using your current emotional patterns and perceptions of self to create your present life circumstances. In fact, life conforms to us at all times. It exists for one purpose and one purpose only: to be a constant metaphor for who we feel we are in each and every moment so that we may connect to our *loveseeds* and continue to evolve.

In essence, I alone get to decide the meaning of the hummingbird visitation. My previous inquiry about hummingbirds taught me that this tiny bird of joy symbolizes great courage, determination, flexibility, and adaptability. Though only a few ounces in weight, the hummingbird has the courage of a lion, representing fearlessness and lightness-of-being. Hummingbirds take a 3,000-mile journey each way during the annual migration from Central America to as far north as Alaska, facing countless challenges along the way. Some actually fly 500 miles over open water with no food to get to their destination. They return to the very same gardens year after year on their great migration journeys. They are territorial and boldly defend their territory, symbolizing the need to be feisty when necessary to protect your boundaries and what is yours.

I believe that the hummingbird's message is for me and for you, dear readers, for after all, we are deeply connected. The message: you are called to embark on a great journey in which you will face new challenges and new ideas and boundaries of the mind. When your new ways of being are challenged by others, be sure you know what is yours and what is not. You may find this journey daunting and difficult at times, and you must persevere and say "yes," believing it will be done. Hummingbird is the ambassador of this very special magic of believing anything is possible.

You must move back and forth between the past and the future by living fully in the present moment. Hummingbird teaches us to go beyond time and to see that what happened in the past and what may happen in the future is not nearly as important as what is occurring now, and that as we hover in the moment, we can drink deeply of the nectar of life, which we need for our journey. **We were born to have a big, bold, daring adventure in this life, and to feel the joy of our own aliveness throughout the experience.**

This is the transmission I received from hummingbird, along with many other truths. The spiritual teacher Radhanath Swami says, "Mother Nature is always speaking. She speaks in the language understood within the peaceful mind of the sincere observer."

Who, what, why, how, and which?

As the sincere observer of this experience, who, then, was this part of me that was not afraid? What was happening to the part of me that was afraid? Why did I have to make a choice, and how did I do that? Which one is actually Kathleen? Let us take a look at what actually happens when we perceive. After all, if a miracle is a shift in perception, then being able to choose *how* we see things is a potent tool in the co-creator's toolbox.

The body has a lot of skin in the game. Really, the body depends on us to keep it alive. It will tell us to run at the slightest whisper of danger, unless we let it know who is running the show. My initial fear when the bird came close to my face was body-based, and I really had no control over actually feeling the fear. I only had a choice as to what I did about it. So much for the myth of fearlessness!

We look out at the world through our senses, mainly seeing, hearing, feeling, tasting, and smelling, as well as countless other receptors within us that download information through electrical nerve impulses in the brain and that then render impressions in the mind. Your brain is physical; your mind is not. Together, I refer to them as bodymind, and they are very much like the hard drive and software of a sophisticated computer. Unlike a real computer, if the energy patterns coming into the bodymind are disturbing or dangerous, a person reacts by resisting and defending, and energy becomes blocked within the bodymind. The simplest word for this is *stress*. You begin to feel uncomfortable, constrained, or maybe the opposite—out of control. You feel off-balance. Somewhere, you are resisting your experience.

Was it my mind or my heart that decided to open? My mind was involved in this decision, informed by my heart. There was my bodily reaction of fear that caused my heart to pump wildly, and there was another part of me that was not afraid and made a split-second decision to open. In *Blue Truth: A Spiritual Guide to Life & Death and Love & Sex*, spiritual teacher David Deida says, "Whether you open or close makes all the difference to whether you feel trapped by your situation or open as an offering of love."

I call this part of me that decided to open the *Witness,* which is very distinct from the part of me that was afraid of losing my eyes. I will elaborate more about this *Witness* throughout this book. For now, think of it as a silent observer who does not judge the experience, but simply witnesses it from the consciousness available to the person. I had been cultivating this aspect of my being through meditation and prayer for over 40 years, which did not absolve me from the fear, but allowed me to transcend it. This is a skill we all need to nurture if we are to protect ourselves from the slings and arrows of life.

When we cultivate the *Witness* who is able to view the larger picture and see with the eyes of the heart, we can easily tap into the archetypal realm, which is what I did. In a lucid moment of just the right neurons firing, I realized the epic nature of this quiet moment alone on my friend's back porch. I experienced myself as a flower being pollinated by the hummingbird. In another synchronistic moment, when I shared the morning's event with my friend Lavon later that day, she declared me to be like a trumpet.

The symbolic meaning of trumpet is of considerable consequence in the Bible and has signified an alarm of war; a call to assemble or a command to march. All at once, I was a trumpet flower being pollinated to declare the imperative to cultivate the *loveseed* in all beings. Could this be inflated hubris, madness, or me elevating my experience to epic realness? No, no, and yes. I felt humbled, incredibly sane, and utterly blessed at the very heart of the matter.

CHAPTER 4

To the Heart of the Matter

"The best and most beautiful things
in the world cannot be seen or even touched—
they must be felt with the heart."
— Helen Keller

The three hearts

Now that you understand how I experienced my morning hummingbird visitation, I want to explain how much my decision to breath into my heart had to do with letting go of the fear. This simplest of acts—consciously breathing into the center of my chest, toward the back near my spine—opened up a doorway through which I stepped into another dimension of consciousness. You may wonder what I'm talking about. After all, the heart is not in the center of the chest, toward the spine. That is true of the physical heart, but there are three hearts with very different functions, all important in unique ways.

The *first heart* rules all things physical and is the actual pump on the left side of your chest that allows you to remain alive in this body. It is deeply connected to the other two hearts. The human heart is the gateway that allows you to access the higher dimensions and is a bridge between your spiritual and your human energies anchored here on Earth. The heart is 500 times more electrically powerful than the brain, and 5,000 times more electromagnetically powerful than the brain. It is truly a power center that entrains all other biological rhythms in your body and allows you to connect to all dimensions of consciousness.

The *second heart* rules all things spiritual and is often called the *heart chakra*. It is a non-physical energy that is in the center of your chest. When the heart chakra is strong and often open in a person's life, she or he is guided out of darkness and toward the light and goodness.

The *third heart* is found in the center of the chest and toward the back of the spine and rules all things. It is the bridge that connects you to all that is. The third heart is the Sacred Heart and is the Divine Flame depicted in representations of the Sacred Heart of Jesus. It rises out of the heart chakra, which in pictures of Christ has thorns, representing the suffering we experience as human beings.

The Sacred Heart is called the Three-fold Heart, as it is comprised of the three-fold flames of gold, pink, and blue light. The pure Divine Feminine ray which relates to our right brain and heart is crystalline pink, possessing the qualities of unconditional Divine Love, compassion, and reverence for all life, and signifies the essence of our **true self.** The pure Divine Masculine ray of energy (relating to our left brain, throat, and heart) is sapphire blue and relates to the power, will, and inner resolve to set the course for one's life, or **true north**.

When the Divine Feminine and Divine Masculine rays of energy are unified and balanced within us, the consciousness of the gold ray is awakened, which is called "Christ consciousness." The gold flame embodies wisdom and illumination, and the ability to discriminate and use the gifts we have been given on the path of our **true calling**. Understand that my use of the term "Christ consciousness" does not have to do with Christianity, which is a religion. It has to do with the higher awareness that is inherent in the *loveseed* of every human being, which is the awareness that Christ embodied and taught.

When all three flames are balanced within us, love, power, and wisdom reign in a person's life. This Violet Flame of transmutation burns away all that is not you so only the true essence of you remains—the seat of the Soul, the part of you that is one with your life's purpose, and from which you can harness the energy of your *loveseed*. Learning to live from this place allows you to live with a sense of grace, no matter what is happening.

Most people are oblivious that this aspect of their being is always there, experiencing everything, as they race from one task to the other in their hectic lives. Being able to intentionally turn down the churn of the mind and turn up the flame of transmutation is a skill you will want to learn if you are to live a life of power and joy.

The Sacred Heart is considered a holy chamber inside you where true prayer takes place. It is a state of deep peace and quiet, connected to Source. Being able to enter this space brings with it the gifts of alchemy, where you transmute your suffering and sorrow, and your fear and anger.

Before conception, your Soul was in non-physical form. The soul substance is composed of adamantine particles, taken from the Greek word *adamas*, meaning invincible and referring to something extremely hard or unyielding. It could also be indicating something clear and brilliant, like a diamond.

When the term "particle" appears with adamantine, it derives from quantum theory and describes all fundamental, subatomic particles that form all the elements in the Universe. These particles assemble the atoms of all the original substances such as oxygen, hydrogen, and iron and are the basis of everything that exists. Imagine that! They are the smallest particles that cannot be divided any further—crystalline particles of infinity that store the potential to manifest any original element or substance.

The exchange of adamantine particles is the exchange of life, which goes on throughout existence. They are particles of infinity that are irreducible, fundamental, and utterly elemental. Not only do they comprise our body, but also the wind and the ocean and everything about us, under the guidance of love. There is an ongoing exchange of these particles throughout eternity. They belong both to the infinite world and the limited realm of physical existence. They are Source or seed energy.

What this means is that every manifestation in the third dimension of form emerges from the infinite expanse of Source energy or Light composed of unlimited potential. It is another way of saying that before you were born, you were with God—you were one with God/Spirit/Absolute Being. **It is so important to see that the essence of who you are is under the command of love, in all dimensions.**

Until now, understanding and utilizing these particles was for priests and mystics of the highest order; for saints who could perform miracles. **When the Sacred Heart is activated and central to your life, it serves as a magnet for exactly those adamantine particles to form in the perfect way that will forward the flowering of your loveseed**. As you begin to magnetize adamantine particles from the infinitely-abundant Universe that is available to you, your role as co-creator in your own life is strengthened.

When Christ told his disciples to distribute the loaves and fishes among the people, and one became two and on and on until all the people were fed, he was calling on the power of the Sacred Heart to command the adamantine particles to multiply. What is more, in John 14:12 NIV he said, "Very truly I tell you, whoever believes in me will do the works I have been doing, and they will do even greater things than these, because I am going to the Father."

Seeing with the eyes of the heart

As the Lower Heart or heart chakra remains open more and more—in spite of and in part due to suffering and circumstances—the upper heart begins to take over. The shift in perception that takes place when the Sacred Heart begins to flower is the true enlightenment. You begin to see the Divine everywhere. This seeing with the eyes of the heart is a choice we make that entirely shifts our destiny.

I recall that shift happening so powerfully for me while living in Peru. I had already lived in three places, and each one had its challenges: rats; freezing water in the shower; neighbors who partied all night. I was finally settled into my latest flat and feeling so lonely and defeated by all I had endured. Getting my phone installed had taken a month, and my internet failed to work most times I needed it. First-world problems in the third world present opportunities for awakening at every turn.

It was a Saturday and I needed to go to the bigger market to stock up on food for the week, which meant taking a cab through a section of town that I perceived at the time to be "disgusting and dirty." I had heard myself say that a few times to a friend, commenting on why "they" could not do a better job of picking up trash in Peru. At that time, I had a heart that seemed to open and close at whim, triggered by things I didn't like. I had not yet cultivated the space inside me to accept all things with grace.

It was a day like any other; one in which I struggled with being so alone in a foreign land, simultaneously requiring and resisting the solitude. I was surrounded by beauty and poverty and was deeply saddened by the news of Hurricane Katrina in the United States. I questioned if I should go to New Orleans to help, as I had been trained in such things. I was angry at my country's government for going to war, and now this neglect of humanity was breaking my heart. I spent a great deal of time in prayer and meditation in the weeks before but continued to flip-flop between being grateful and awake to angry and despairing.

As I sat in the back of the jerking cab, annoyed at the driver's aggression, I laughed at how aggressive I myself had been lately, complaining about every little thing. I was aware of my misery and that I was resisting the joyful and awake state I longed for. I sat back, rested in the *Witness* aspect of my awareness, and breathed a huge sigh of surrender into my heart.

Suddenly and quietly, the way I perceived all things changed. I felt an expansion similar to the experience with the hummingbird, and my heart burst open. I looked at the garbage, filth, and all the other "annoying" things, and I saw a soft, warm light everywhere. I did not see filth, but beauty, as love emanated from me and back to me from everything I witnessed. I was seeing with the eyes of the heart—the Sacred Heart.

I recall giving the driver a big tip and prepared to enter the crowded market where people were packed like sardines. I had enough presence of mind to clutch my purse more tightly, since "gringas" in Peru were often robbed by locals, yet I did not see anyone as a potential threat. I felt "in love" with everyone there, smiling and merging on the level of the heart.

There is only one Sacred Heart, and it belongs to all of us. When the Sacred heart is activated, you realize your Oneness with all things. To use an old term from my hippie days, I was "blissed out." I had been lifted out of my local human misery to the world of the gods.

I realized that I had been given a gift and that while it seemed to come out of nowhere, my prayer and meditation of the months prior had paved the way for this experience of unity consciousness. I had planted the seeds of this moment, and the flowering was magnificent. The expanded state where I seemed to live on higher ground while remaining connected to everyone and everything around me lasted two weeks. Even after I seemed to "come down to earth," I was different. The polarities of my joy and misery seemed to merge, and I was more "integrated," to use a term from Carl Jung.

Again, my willingness to surrender my judging mind—as I had surrendered my fearful mind with the hummingbird—opened up a portal for me to step through into an entirely different dimension of consciousness. Each time, I received a precious gift when I was able to get to the heart of the matter.

Question your beliefs

Sometimes the solution to your problem is not what you think it is.

When Pope Francis visited Philadelphia, he gave from his heart and spoke truth that challenged the "unconscious acquiescence" to living a superficial life where we are slaves to our beliefs. When he spoke of the mother who came to him bemoaning that her 34-year-old son still lives at home and has no direction, his advice was, "Stop ironing his clothes."

Sometimes it's like that. Pope Francis's recommendation to this mother who is enslaved to her belief that she must tolerate behavior in her son that leads to her own resentment said nothing about what the son needed to change. He focused her on her own issue, not her son's. Remember, there are many factors involved in this illusion called the *Trance*.

To review: We have all developed a false self that masquerades for who we think we are. And then there is that *blind spot* that causes us to believe that things happening now are the cause of our problems, when in truth, the cause began long ago. The greatest melodramas of all time arise out of this confusion, which must be cleared up if you are to live a life connected to your *loveseed* and thus, your essential aliveness. If we have covered up who we truly are, it makes sense that if we take the *Path of Zero* to let go of what is not us to get to our True Self, our *loveseed*, we could see more clearly and feel alive and joyful again.

But why take this journey at all? What could possibly motivate anyone to follow a path that involves giving up things and changes that we cannot anticipate, when there are plenty of quick fixes to be had? Besides, life is already so busy and fast and challenging. Who needs to think about taking a journey that gets you to nothing? Why ride in a lowly Fiat when you could ride in a high-end Mercedes?

"Why" is the wrong question to ask if you want an explanation. "Why is my wife such a nag?" or even worse, the generalized question that is really a complaint: "Why can't men just take initiative around the house?" Would you really believe me or anyone if you were told, "When you act like a teenager you elicit a nagging response in your wife," or "When you treat your husband like a child, you end up getting uncooperative behavior."

That may be enough to shift some of us, but believe me, knowing this does not necessarily change a thing if we have not learned to choose a different path. And that involves creating different neural pathways in our brains, which means making the connection with the other person more important than being right. You cannot explain your way through such a profound shift that changes even your brain chemistry. This is the courageous work of the heart.

What good does it do you to know that the reason you still feel like a fraud and failure after four PhDs and several books published has something to do with the fact that your father wanted you to become a lawyer like him, but you became a professor, and you never felt fully accepted by him after that? Or that your total lack of fulfillment comes from the fact that you did become a lawyer like your father, when you really wanted to become a preacher or a musician? After having someone else explain why, does it make a bit of difference to the pain you feel on a daily basis?

Would you believe me if I told you the reason why it is wise to take this journey of transformation is that the call has gone out that humanity is in trouble and that some of us volunteered to turn the tide of self-destruction? And that you may be one of those who answered the call but lost that memory when you came to Earth? Some will laugh, and some will resonate with that. So, my telling you why it is wise for you to embark on a path that seems at first to take you to nothing may offer you a well-deserved explanation, but you must dig deeper than that. You must ask yourself why YOU would want to put the effort in when life is already such a struggle and a balancing act.

In fact, I recommend questioning all "authority" and coming to know what is true for yourself as a way of life. That is the only way you will begin to know and live as your *True Self*. Remember that I am a trumpet, a messenger, here to deliver a message. I am not here to convince you but to inspire you to listen deeply to yourself. The walls come down, but it is you who must step into freedom.

Why get to Zero?

If you are going to ask "Why?" you may as well get to the heart of the matter. It is my intention to share many pieces of wisdom and knowledge with you so that your mind can serve your heart and you can understand more clearly in order to answer the question of "Why?" for yourself.

Begin by questioning YOUR motivations. Ask yourself what fuels you to do anything. I do an exercise with people asking them repeatedly, "Why?" Someone identifies an issue or problem, and the line of question-and-answer goes something like this and brings very similar results with person after person. In this case, I am asking Lisa, who is still struggling with her inability to regulate her eating:

"Why do you continue to overeat carbohydrates that spike your blood sugar?"

"Because I feel better for a little while."

"Why do you want to feel better?"

"Because I don't feel happy." (Often, tears begin to well up.)

"Why don't you feel happy?"

"Because my mother always criticizes me."

"Why do you feel unhappy when your mother criticizes you?"

"Because she doesn't love me."

"Why does your mother not love you?"

"Because I am unlovable." (Many tears now.)

"Why are you unlovable?"

"Because I hate my baby sister."

"Why do you hate your baby sister?"

"Because she gets all the love."

"Why does she get all the love?"

"Because I don't deserve it." (Deep sadness is usually evident by now.)

"Why don't you deserve to be loved?"

"Because I am just not good. I am unlovable."

When we continually arrive at the place where Lisa's belief in her own unlovability arises over and over, I know we have come to the beginning of the real problem. It is not that Lisa or anyone is inherently unlovable, but that she *believes* that. We are at the underlying belief that leads to the feeling that taking the *Path of Zero* helps you discover and release.

The true starting point for Lisa's problematic *behaviors* is that she *feels* insignificant and worthless. So often, a destructive or unhealthy activity is repeated over and over to keep us from feeling the original pain. In Lisa's case, I did not have to hypnotize her, nor regress her to childhood. I only had to start by identifying the symptom that's created so much suffering in her life.

We identified a belief that led Lisa to bury her *loveseed*, thus leading her to use food to soothe the pain of felt rejection. We touched Lisa's deep shame and feelings of insignificance, and we have touched the hope of healing. This pain is the original wound, which is an actively-running subconscious program in her psyche and a denial of the love she longs for. Beneath it is her salvation, her *loveseed*, that lives inside the still point of *Zero* in her Sacred Heart. Arriving at this point is the beginning of healing.

This beginning point is nothing new to poets and mystics, and I include myself in that lot, always feeling a bit weird, yet strangely OK with it. Since I was 20, I have carried a quote by T.S. Eliot in my wallet. "East Coker" is my most important "calling card," by which I mean, a clue to my own calling:

We must be still and still moving,

Into another intensity

For a further union, a deeper communion...

In my beginning is my end.

I consumed Eliot's poetry and made a vow to get to the "still point of the turning world" while still alive.

Perhaps that quote by Eliot means little to you, but I bet there is some piece of wisdom that could be considered your "calling card," some declaration that you may have said consciously (or maybe unconsciously). It is a clue to your *true calling*, your *dharma*, which I will share more about in a later chapter.

Back in the day

In a very real sense, I have taken the *Path of Zero* my entire life, surrendering cherished beliefs and even my material wealth at one point, in the service of a greater Mystery than I could ever fully explain. I have done a life review while alive, rather than waiting until my deathbed and having my whole life flash before me, helpless to do anything about it.

Since we are all connected deeply at the core of things, I knew that if I could make sense of my own life, others could benefit from what I have learned. This book is the "deeper communion" my calling card speaks of, and we are living now in "another intensity," as any awake human being can see. In a very real sense, the story of my life and this book were already written before I was born, as was my destiny.

It simply took me until nearly 60 to begin to fully cooperate with my own destiny. It's never too late!

The Path of Zero

In both stories I have shared with you, there were two essential ingredients for the shift in perspective to occur. First, I connected to my *Witness,* and next I shifted my awareness to the Sacred Heart. The felt experience of the *Witness* is toward the back and top of the head, and the felt experience of the Sacred Heart is in the center of the chest toward the spine. It is a sacred portal, the intersection of mortal and immortal life in each of us. I call the movement from the *Witness* to the Sacred Heart the *Path of Zero*, and it requires that you totally surrender all that is not you (ego, false self) so that you can allow life to flow through you and no longer resist that which is. **It is the most important journey you will ever take and leads directly to your loveseed.** This journey is not measured in distance, but in the quality of your attention and intention, and unlike other journeys you have taken, you must unpack your bags **before** you take the *Path of Zero*.

The sweet spot of Zero

At the heart of the *Path of Zero* lies a gem: *Zero Point.* This figure-eight sweet spot is where the lines of spiraling energy cross; a place where yin/yang polarity ceases. Charged fields of positive and negative are neutralized here. In an article on his website entitled *528 Hz and ZERO POINT ENERGY: The Cure for What Ails Humanity,*

Leonard G. Horowitz says, "The energy sourcing from *Zero Point* theoretically flows in at least 36 dimensions."

This *Zero Point* is also inextricably connected to your personal heart, and to your life's calling—that which you are here to manifest as only you can. This is why we so often feel our calling as something "tugging at our heartstrings," because it actually is, and when we do not heed that call, we block the spiritual energy that would be released if we did. When we connect to this spiritual energy, we connect to yet another heart, a bigger intelligence—the *Global Heart*—as our personal energy radiates out in 36 dimensions; not directions, but dimensions. You feel the pain of the world, and you are called to flow infinite love toward it, which connects you intimately to all things; to a deeper communion with life. This is what allows a single human being to be a mighty force for good, which, as I've already stated, is so needed on the planet right now.

The great unraveling

Earlier I asked the question "Why bother to take the journey to *Zero*?" Let's take a look at what is happening when it comes to happiness and fulfillment today.

A June 2013 Gallup Poll revealed that 70% of Americans hate their jobs or have "checked out" of them. The number of people who qualified for Social Security Disability (SSDI) for mental disorders increased nearly 2.5 times between 1987 and 2007. In her *New York Review of Books* article, "The Epidemic of Mental Illness:

Why?", Marcia Angell states, "There has been a thirty-five-fold increase in the same for children." In 2011, the U.S. Centers for Disease Control and Prevention (CDC) reported that antidepressant use in the United States has increased nearly 400% in the last two decades, making antidepressants the most frequently used class of medications by Americans between the ages of 18 and 44 years. By 2008, 23% of women aged 40–59 were taking antidepressants. On May 3, 2013, the CDC reported that the suicide rate among Americans aged 35–64 increased more than 28% between 1999 and 2010. The United States is less than 5% of the world's population, yet uses 80% of the global supply of opioid drugs.

In the course of writing this book, countless mass killings of innocent people have happened in the United States, and more and more often in schools. We have the highest rate of mass killings in the world, not because Americans are more violent than other people, but because the overwhelming pressure of modern life is sending more and more people—particularly alienated young men saturated with the toxic masculinity of the culture—into the margins, and the disowned shadow of our ineffectual and politicized leaders. In fact, the shadow of our entire money-driven culture dwells in the margins where we fail to see them as our own. This shadow is not accidental but is growing out of the refusal of those in power to face and fully feel the dilemma.

Michael Meade addresses the lack of basic mirroring and mentoring that has led to this out-picturing of destruction. In *The Genius Myth* he states, "A society is playing with fire each time it rejects the innate nobility of its youth. For youth not only carry within them the dream of the future, they also tend to act out the imbalances and injustices of society as well as the deep grievances of their communities. Injustices that are not faced inside a culture will eventually be lived out on the streets as a kind of fate."

A numbness has set in, and that is its own form of mental illness leading to further dissociation. No matter how many people die, and no matter how many countless family members' lives are irrevocably altered, the killings keep on happening as long as our leaders make it a "mental illness" issue or, worse yet, a human right based on the Second Amendment. The problem of mental illness is huge, and while many of the killers were in the mental health system, many were not, so it cannot be deflected as a mental illness problem alone.

Every one of the broken individuals committing these mass murders that have escalated over the past several years was isolated and bereft of authentic connection. That is the real mental illness of our times. This is a human and not a political issue, and still the political debate goes on while more innocents die.

We live in a culture where, when you grieve a loss or even for the pain of your past and seek help, you are labeled "depressed" and given medication to suppress a natural feeling that comes from being human. If you are very sensitive and have not learned to handle your own pain, let alone the pain of the world, being alive really is depressing.

I totally agree that there are times when psychotropic medication is a life-saver, as are antibiotics in cases of infection. In both instances, however, their indiscriminate overuse is part of the collective *Trance* that prevents human beings from reclaiming their personal power and getting to the underlying cause of suffering, whether it is physical, emotional, or spiritual. That *Trance* has a profound effect in every aspect of our lives.

Psychology and psychiatry are new "sciences," and diagnostic categories are based on behaviors that made a committee of mental health professionals (mostly middle-aged white males) feel uncomfortable. They are unverified categories that vary from person to person. The training of mental health professionals has not involved helping them or the people they serve to connect to their *loveseed*, so I am not pointing a finger at anyone. It is not about blame, but about seeing what is real. Those who call themselves helpers and healers, whether shamans or medical doctors and nurses, must be able to see the *loveseed* in those they serve, or they will burn out or become ineffective.

In 2010, a former reporter named Robert Whitaker wrote a book called *Mad in America*, which showed the evidence from psychiatry's own research that the drugs being prescribed not only for psychotic disorders, but all so-called "mental illnesses," were causing more harm than good. He found that people diagnosed with depression, bipolar, and schizophrenia and were drugged long-term were losing 12–20 years in life expectancy, and that their conditions were far worse than those who had not been treated.

His findings created a big uproar, and Whitaker was condemned by mainstream medicine and Big Pharma. Remember that Galileo was jailed when he said the Earth was round! The good news is that a group of psychiatrists and other mental health professionals who took Whitaker's findings to heart, had the courage to look at the shadow of medicine right in the eyes and held a conference in Portland, Oregon, in 2011, where the **Foundation for Excellence in Mental Health Care** was formed. Now there is the grassroots movement of change.

On another front, the relatively new science of epigenetics is the study of inheritable changes in gene function that do not involve changes in the DNA sequence. The prefix *epi* means "over, outside of," and implies features that are in addition to the traditional genetic basis for inheritance. It's as if there is a switch that is outside of the genetic circuitry that influences the behaviors of a gene. Trauma, childhood neglect and abuse, having to play a parental role in a family, poor nutrition, exposure to toxic chemicals, exposure to everyday antibiotics and hormones in the food supply and other mainstream synthetic medicine, are among the countless causes of a variety of symptoms that are labeled mental illness.

I am not suggesting you throw out your medications if you are taking them, particularly because of the negative effects of withdrawal. What I am suggesting is that you revisit the reason you sought help and were prescribed medication in the first place. Get in touch with that part of you that wanted to make things better; to be relieved of the pain. Find a guide to take the inner journey back to your *True Self*, which you can do while taking medication.

I believe it is time for a serious multidisciplinary taskforce of mental health professionals, law enforcement officers, and communities to address the issue of loneliness, alienation, and shame—a mass effort to help people connect to their *loveseeds*, which requires that people connect deeply with one another. Remember that to come to know your *loveseed*, you must first be reflected by another. This involves genuine connection to others, and that is not accomplished via social media and the trance of technology substituting for genuine connection.

Though I am passionate about these things and am tempted to dive deeply into possible solutions, right now I am here to answer the question "Why bother to do the deeper work of taking the *Path of Zero* to connect with your *loveseed*?" I believe the statistics above scream something really important at us that has to do with answering that question.

A collective spiritual emergency

Whether life today is more difficult than it was a generation ago or not, something has happened to our expectations. One of the dark sides of our lightning-speed digital world is that people have become accustomed to a strange new belief that we should be able to have whatever we want, when we want it. There is no holding any tension and delaying gratification, but rather increased expectation that life should automatically be fulfilling and pleasurable.

Narcissism is the disease of our times, and we have all become immune to the effect of one of its main features, which is entitlement, confusing it with the deep and abiding intrinsic worth that each person has. We forget that we are not "entitled" to cable TV, but that we have earned the money to choose and pay for it, and when it is not working as it should, it's not the end of the world and there's no reason to blast the person on the other end of the help line.

We now have a case of mass entitlement that comes from falling into the *Trance* and believing that the things we are grasping for will actually fill the emptiness in our hearts. Here is what Bruce Levine—a psychiatrist and outspoken activist who speaks out on the Big Pharma corruption of psychiatry—has to say in an article on his website entitled *Why the Rise of Mental Illness? Pathologizing Normal, Adverse Drug Effects, and a Peculiar Rebellion*:

"For many of us, society has become increasingly alienating, isolating, and insane, and earning a buck means more degrees, compliance, ass-kissing, shit-eating, and inauthenticity. So, we want to rebel. However, many of us feel hopeless about the possibility of either our own escape from societal oppression or that political activism can create societal change. So, many of us, especially young Americans, rebel by what is commonly called mental illness."

In the words of two of my earliest mentors, Stanislav and Christina Grof, people are having "spiritual emergencies" at an untold rate. They were referring to the fact that in 1989, when they wrote the book *Spiritual Emergency*, increasing numbers of people involved in personal transformation were experiencing crises as the process of growth and change became chaotic and overwhelming. In a sense, people were being catapulted onto the *Path of Zero*, though not consciously, where their sense of identity began to break down, their old values no longer held true, and the very ground of their personal reality was radically shifting.

I was one of those people, and thankfully found the Grofs during that time and chose to feel my way through, rather than remain in the *Trance*. New realms of mystical and spiritual experience opened up for me, along with confusion, a huge disruption to my marriage, and tremendous anxiety that I struggled to stay ahead of. Thankfully, I had a therapist who was able to distinguish my upheaval from mental illness, and my transformational crisis became the doorway to an entire new reality for me, as well as an entirely new life purpose. This was my preparation to become a transpersonal psychotherapist.

Now, 30 years later, we are in the midst of a collective spiritual emergency, and it is happening to people who have not necessarily chosen a conscious path of growth and transformation. **The work of Stan and Christina Grof revealed that within the crisis of individual spiritual emergency lies the promise of spiritual emergence and renewal, and that is still true today**. The solution is still the same and goes back to the personal imperative for each of us to connect to our *loveseed*.

At this point you might say that a very good reason to take the *Path of Zero* to connect you to your *loveseed* is because if you don't choose, life will catapult you onto that path anyway. You can go kicking and screaming, or you can make the choice to embark on the path right here, right now. It may indeed be the most important decision you ever make in your life and the life of all beings, because what you choose affects everyone else.

While we are here on Earth, accessing the pure aliveness of our *loveseeds* is an act of love for the world. Just as everything in your spirit reflects in your body, everything in mass consciousness is reflected in the Earth we all claim. If we could reclaim the divine capacities we were born with, we would be able to be at one with the soul of all creatures; a living offering of love sourced through the Sacred Heart. Part of reclaiming our divine capabilities is knowing that we're "enough."

CHAPTER 5

On Being Enough

"In the coming world, they will not ask me:
'Why were you not Moses?' They will ask me:
'Why were you not Zusya?'"
— Rabbi Zusya

Each of us is doing the best we can

I truly believe that you, like most people, are doing the very best you can. I also know that when life presents you with deep betrayal and loss and the emotional mountains and valleys of everyday life, the opportunity to know who you truly are aside from your conditioning is at its peak. The opportunity to drop the false self and get real is right in front of you.

People come to me in the heat of opportunities that most often present as crises. "I've had it. Nothing makes sense any more. After all these years... after all I gave to this kid. I've had it. That kid is out of my life." Or, "I am done.

I have had it. He is a hopeless idiot. I am getting a divorce at last." This is what I hear from good people who come to me when they are in pain from a breakup, fight, loss, child's addiction, or any one of a number of stressors that tear at the fabric of even a stable life. They are angry, often at God, and want revenge. This is impotent rage.

When someone lashes out from that place, they are "offending from the victim position," as Terrance Real, author of *The New Rules of Marriage,* says. From the same book, he writes, "I believe that offending from the victim position accounts for ninety percent of the world's violence. Whether the form it takes is a cold silence or an unkind word between two partners, or it's the act of a disenfranchised, angry criminal who feels entitled to violate our civil code, or a seemingly endless cycle of violence between fractious countries or ethnic groups, violence at all levels is fueled by the RIGHTEOUS ANGER of the victim."

As a psychotherapist, I concur. We can feel defeated and remain caught in the drama of our lives with no ability to see the larger picture, unable to make meaning out of any of it. When this happens, we allow the unconscious behavior of others to personally wound us, and we suffer unconsciously, which is a precursor to repetition. The same neural pathways in the brain are being fired, over and over, literally creating a rut. We can slide into one failed relationship after another. We can experience chronic illness that countless doctors cannot source. We can be bright and have so much to offer, and yet be so broke we cannot even pay for healthcare.

If you've struggled with health, finances, or relationships, it's understandable that you'd question the meaning of your life. You may have even fallen into the victim role for a while, or you may be stuck there now—broke, broken, or broken down. It's at such times that people come to me with the expectation that I can help them sort things out and ease the pain. What I know is that each and every person comes to me for a sacred reason that I must be open to discovering with them. They are self-absorbed and need to be for a while.

One of the reasons I can truly help them is that I have chosen the *Path of Zero* and made meaning of my suffering—which has been plenty—so that I can consciously use the slings and arrows of life to poke holes in the veil of illusion that shrouds life on planet Earth. The other reason is that I know beyond a shadow of a doubt that there is a *loveseed* in every one of them, and I know the pain they are feeling because they have lost that vital connection.

The truth is that the cycle of abuse, neglect, and violence continues to happen in families every day, and victimization is real. I have a dear friend who suffered the most horrific childhood of anyone I know, and yet she does not offend from the victim's position. She is deeply compassionate and has become a healer herself. She carries the archetypal energy of the "wounded healer," and has done the work of transforming the pain and suffering of her wounding to helping others heal. You may wonder what determines the difference between my friend and the countless other victimized human beings who continue to perpetrate abuse on others. A deeper exploration into the phenomenon of narcissism will shed some light on this issue.

The real story about narcissism

Jack was a handsome, bright, and highly-defensive man who came to me in pain over his wife having an affair with another man. The usual word for Jack would be "arrogant," but that judgment does not serve a psychotherapist any more than the label "narcissistic" does, if you to fail see with the eyes of the heart past that "suit of armor."

Jack's wife had been his stalwart, his beacon in the storm. She was fed up, and rightly so. Jack had been drinking, absent, and totally absorbed in his private reveries of days of glory when he was an adventurer of the free world, while Tina raised four young children and held a full-time job. He sat down on my office couch and said, "*I* am a Narcissist. That is what *I* have been told, and *I* believe it is true, so you should know that about me" (emphasis on the "I").

"You may or may not be. I don't place a lot of weight on those terms, but I can tell you were wounded and feel the need to defend yourself," I replied.

"Yes, I have been, and they are horrors you don't even want to know about. Thank you. That somehow feels better than a label. Now we can continue."

For a flicker of a moment there was a glimmer of his light as he let me see that "chink in the armor" of the narcissistic defense that locks people in their own chambers of shame. It was the crack he needed to peek out from, and also where the light gets in. He went back into hiding for a long time after that, but we had made the connection.

Jack had suffered a childhood of both horror and coldness, a potentially debilitating combination, and had deeply buried his *loveseed*. He used his quick and acerbic wit and verbal eloquence to keep everyone but his wife at a distance, and he was desperate for connection.

Having read about Jack, consider this definition from the Mayo Clinic: "Narcissistic personality disorder is a mental disorder in which people have an inflated sense of their own importance, a deep need for admiration and a lack of empathy for others. But behind this mask of ultra-confidence lies a fragile self-esteem that's vulnerable to the slightest criticism. A narcissistic personality disorder causes problems in many areas of life, such as relationships, work, school, or financial affairs. You may be generally unhappy and disappointed when you're not given the special favors or admiration you believe you deserve. Others may not enjoy being around you, and you may find your relationships unfulfilling."

I would replace "narcissistic personality disorder" with "narcissism," as there are certainly degrees and various manifestations, and in the world of mental health, a personality disorder is considered somewhat of a life sentence. The distinction between narcissistic personality disorder versus narcissistic style simply has to do with the degree to which the person is capable of becoming aware of themselves and tolerating the grief necessary to shed the suit of armor. We need to get real to heal. Some folks have a hard time with that, and the mere thought of becoming vulnerable is too bitter a pill to swallow after all they have already suffered.

It is essential that you understand this: **Any path of healing or transformation requires a letting go, and a grieving of what was, to allow what is coming into existence.** Many people do not know how to be with that grief. It is the grief that arises when you realize that you have been living separate from your true self, from your *loveseed*, and often there is a fierce rage associated with it. If you lived in the layers of defenses, far from your *essence*, you must be able to touch into the emotions that have been repressed and feel them without judgment. It is the only way to live as your true self, without which there continues to be deep pain and so much shame that you do not have the courage to live authentically. Community minister and law enforcement chaplain Kate Braestrup says, "Walk fearlessly into the house of mourning. For grief is just love squaring up to its oldest enemy, and after all these mortal human years love is up to the challenge."

This deep sense of shame and unworthiness at the root of narcissism has different expressions. On the one hand, it is represented by what we classically consider narcissistic—grandiosity and braggadocio. In this case, there is no felt experience of shame, but rather, entitlement—the shame is disowned, leading the person to behave shamelessly and often cruelly to others. There is no consideration of other people, except for how they can be used as a source of supply. These people are split off from their shame, their pain, and their sense of deep despair and unworthiness, and often get into relationships with someone who carries or expresses those disowned feelings. They blame others if things go wrong. At its extreme, this is sociopathology, where every choice the person makes is based on the calculated attempt to win and remain on top. The question is always "What's in it for me?" Nothing about the person can be trusted, for they lack empathy for others and are alienated from their own goodness.

The other side of the coin of this type of narcissism is evidenced in the person who feels defeated by life, filled with shame and doubt, and carries the blame for everything. This is often expressed by a person in relationship with the more grandiose individual, but the reality is that this is the "shadow" aspect of the narcissist—the part that he has constructed an intricate defense system to avoid, and for good reason. There is a depth of self-loathing that becomes debilitating if it breaks through, and thus the need for the "split" in the personality long ago. Because so much is disowned, finding people in their lives who can carry the blame or the ideal of themselves is elemental to the narcissistic defense. This is classically gender based, with men expressing grandiosity and women expressing unworthiness, but I have seen many couples where the reverse is true. It is always sad and it is most often ugly, as it is a toxic dance of power and powerlessness involving projection and disowning parts of the self.

An all-too-common example of this is when a woman who is considered a "love addict" is in relationship with a man who is considered a "narcissist." She grew up serving as a mirror to a parent, often a mother who was lonely and needy, while dad was busy working, drinking or philandering. It could also be the reverse, where the man's needs took precedence. He grew up with a parent or parents who only mirrored the parts of him that looked good, or not at all. Neither of them was ever seen for the child they once were, and their *loveseeds* became hidden in different ways. The drama that unfolds in their lives is mythic, not unlike the myths of old that tell the archetypal stories of human history. These myths exist so we can learn from the grand mistakes of the gods and other human beings who play out well-worn patterns.

The story of Narcissus and Echo

Relevant to this understanding of narcissism is the myth of Narcissus, which is still being played out on the world stage every day. Many people know about the myth of Narcissus, the beautiful and conceited young man from whom the term *narcissism* derived. There are different versions of his demise. One is that Narcissus plunges a dagger into his own heart as he called out a final goodbye to his own reflection. Other versions of the myth have him staring at his own reflection for all eternity, while his body withers away.

Narcissus had his moment of awakening when he became aware of himself. This was the moment he could have chosen to become the hero of his own life. He became a *Witness* to himself and opened to the grief that he could never have the perfect love he had imagined, but he could not stay with that. He did not know how to grieve, for he had never done so in his life but rather used others to feel the pain he refused to surrender to. He played out the ultimate drama of control, where the ego refuses to live if it cannot have what it wants. He never found his *loveseed*, for he never learned how to tolerate his own disappointment. Instead, he lived his life inflicting such feelings onto others.

Archetypal dramas like this one are patterns that affect people's lives more than they realize. The themes repeat over and over. In Western psychology this tendency to repeat the same drama over and over is called the "repetition compulsion," and is actually at attempt to "get it right" each time; to heal the wounds of childhood by finally finding the solution to the original painful dilemma of feeling unloved. Remember, you are not here to "get it right," but to be who you truly are.

I once worked with a woman who had married five addicted men—four alcoholics and one gambler—until she came to me for help. Yes, her father was an alcoholic and her mother a codependent martyr-like woman. She came in saying, "I want off the wheel." I knew what she meant. In Buddhism this repetition is called the Wheel of Samsara and it turns over and over, lifetime after lifetime, now victim, now perpetrator, now rescuer, over and over again, until we accumulate enough wisdom to step off the wheel. Consciousness and the three qualities of the Violet Flame—wisdom, courage, and love—are what allow us to step off the Wheel of Samsara and claim our role as co-creators who possess the power to effect tremendous change.

If you look at reality TV and the wider culture today, you can see that the lessons are not being learned but replayed, over and over, in dramas of control and helplessness, revenge and pure apathy. At the bottom of it all is the deep shame that must first become conscious to be surrendered.

Unpacking the bags of shame

I have referred to shame several times, as well as shamelessness, which is generally thought to be a quality of a psychopathic personality—having no conscience about doing horrific things. We do not need to look to psychopaths to witness the ravages of both shame and shamelessness but can find it in the lives of really good people who have been caught in the grip of shame's debilitating despair, myself included.

In *Power vs. Force,* psychiatrist Dr. David R. Hawkins has created a tool that he calls the "Map of Consciousness."

	Level	Scale (Log of)	Emotion	Process	Life-View
P O W E R	Enlightenment	700-1,000	Ineffable	Pure Consciousness	Is
	Peace	600	Bliss	Illumination	Perfect
	Joy	540	Serenity	Transfiguration	Complete
	Love	500	Reverence	Revelation	Benign
	Reason	400	Understanding	Abstraction	Meaningful
	Acceptance	350	Forgiveness	Transcendence	Harmonious
	Willingness	310	Optimism	Intention	Hopeful
	Neutrality	250	Trust	Release	Satisfactory
	Courage	200	Affirmation	Empowerment	Feasible
F O R C E	Pride	175	Dignity (Scorn)	Inflation	Demanding
	Anger	150	Hate	Aggression	Antagonistic
	Desire	125	Craving	Enslavement	Disappointing
	Fear	100	Anxiety	Withdrawal	Frightening
	Grief	75	Regret	Despondency	Tragic
	Apathy	50	Despire	Abdication	Hopeless
	Guilt	30	Blame	Destruction	Condemnation (Evil)
	Shame	20	Humiliation	Elimination	Miserable

Hawkins calibrated the energy level of the various human emotions and found shame to be energetically at the very lowest rung of the scale of consciousness. It is a force that accompanies more human misery than any other. The lower end of the scale is associated with lower vibrational frequencies: lower power, lower health, less love, and less abundance. Most of us generally avoid this frequency at all costs. However, **it is by consciously touching your own shame with deeply-felt forgiveness and love that you truly heal**. You do this by feeling and surrendering each feeling in a progressive movement up the scale to courage and beyond. Courage is the threshold of transformation, and to get there we must even have the courage to feel our own shame.

When we hide our shame from ourselves, it causes us to live in exile from our true selves, from our *loveseeds*, because we hide it from others and never receive the reflection back that we really need. All humans acquire this complex emotional response during early development. It is not necessarily a symptom of illness or pathology and, in fact, in some situations it would be abnormal if we didn't experience it. The foremost modern researcher and speaker on the subject, in her website article "Shame vs. Guilt," Brene Brown, says that guilt is adaptive and helpful, and helps us live according to our values, whereas shame leads us to believe we are flawed and unworthy of love.

Research suggests that guilt is in place from around the ages of three to six years, while shame occurs much earlier, from fifteen months to three years or even sooner, causing the very young child to feel threatened about its survival. If the infant perceives Mom or Dad as rejecting—and we now know how sensitive young children are—a bodily-felt sense of shame and not "fitting in" begins to take over the child's young system. This is terrifying to a child.

Imagine how magnified this is when the parents truly are disdaining, rejecting, abusing, and contemptuous. The young child has not developed the boundaries to discern what is real and true. As I mentioned in an earlier chapter, this happens to male infants more than to females, causing the need for males to adapt and develop a false self far earlier than females. Instead, the shame begins to get buried and brands the nervous system of the child, scorching with its intensely-heated energy, leaving scar tissue and the experience of something being wrong with self.

When we have done something wrong, as in the case of guilt, we can make amends, and it does not define who we are. But in the case of shame, our whole sense of self is annihilated. It often appears that there is no way back to being fully human, and in extreme cases, numbness takes over. In the absence of feelings, we feel separate, no longer connected to other human beings, and it becomes easy to objectify those around us and to inflict pain. When this happens to men, the combination of their feelings of helplessness and testosterone can lead to expressions of rage that are tremendously destructive on a physical level. And it is equally true that women wreak havoc on the very people they love when they are gripped in the clutches of shame and withhold love and attention in order to silence others for their own disowned feelings of self-loathing.

There is an instinctual desire to discharge the toxic feelings of shame and project them outward onto others—husbands, children, and others who may have what we want. Disowned shame is the root of all violence. When this happens, we act out of our own narcissistic wounds of not being seen, heard, and understood for who we really are and we inflict the same on others. When we do this to our children, we are passing down the unconsciousness from our parents on to our own children.

Back to Jack

I remember the day Jack arrived early to his appointment, before his wife. His head hung down as he sank into my couch. Slowly, he looked up with a pleading look of anger, his hands gripping the air as if trying to get a handle on his untenable plight.

"Kathleen, I just want to feel human. All I want is to feel human."

Jack had witnessed such sadistic violence as a child that he, like so many other un-mothered adult children, could not tolerate his feelings and numbed himself with alcohol. The year he willed himself sober was the "year from hell," according to both his wife and him. Without the pseudo-warmth of the brew, Jack experienced the depth of shame he felt inside and the white-hot rage that had built up over time, hidden from view. The cruelty he witnessed as a child left scars in his psyche, and Jack displaced his impotent rage onto his wife, leaving scars in their marriage.

As mentioned earlier, Alice Miller is an outspoken Swiss psychologist and psychoanalyst who is noted for her books on parental child abuse as well as her departure from psychoanalysis. In an interview for OMNI Publications International she says, "The way we were treated as small children is the way we treat ourselves the rest of our lives: with cruelty or with tenderness and protection. We often impose our most agonizing suffering upon ourselves and, later on, our children."

Miller wrote stories depicting abused and silenced children who later become destructive to themselves and to others. Adolf Hitler was one of the children she studied. He was constantly mistreated by his father, emotionally abandoned by his mother, and lived in a cold and cruel world. He learned to be obedient and to submit to the constant abuse. Need I say more?

Becoming a master on the Path of Zero

The source of our suffering is inside us, and the longer we hold on to the emotions creating the pressure, the longer we suffer. In his book *Letting Go*, David Hawkins says, "Stress results from the accumulated pressure of our repressed and suppressed feelings. The pressure seeks relief, and so external events only trigger what we have been holding down, both consciously and unconsciously. Stress is our emotional reaction to a precipitating factor or stimulus. It is not the external stimulus, then, that is the cause of stress, but our degree of reactivity. The more surrendered we are, the less prone to stress."

Repressed and suppressed emotions, whether conscious or not, must first be witnessed if we are to surrender them. Being able to observe these feelings ourselves—far more than the countless and varied thoughts associated with them—is the key to becoming a more aware and happy human being.

The tendency for human beings to repeat early wounding comes from unwanted emotional learning and underlies most of the emotional and physical symptoms that cause pain and suffering. We call this "implicit" emotional learning, which is not in conscious awareness. This learning entered into memory during experiences that elicited strong emotions, often with family members. The knowledge from these kinds of memories consists of the repetition of templates or patterns that were created and then stored in memory banks that are different from those that house our more conscious or explicit learning. **These emotional learnings were filed according to a feeling tone, not to facts, which is why paying attention to how we feel has many more benefits than trying to figure it out in our heads.**

With each implicit emotional learning there may be thousands of thoughts associated, but a single feeling tone that captures it all. This implicit memory is evidenced in our patterns of attachment, compulsive behaviors, and emotional reactions to external stimuli. It can manifest as anxiety, depression, addictions, fear of intimacy, sexual difficulty, and countless other forms of suffering. It is at the root of racism and other forms of prejudice.

Much has been learned in recent years about the plasticity of the brain and the ability to literally create new neural pathways of joy and acceptance where once there was pain and suffering. The most recent research indicates that consolidated memory can be de-consolidated as the brain unlocks and then relocks synapses encoding a specific memory. This is called *memory reconsolidation* and offers us revolutionary understanding about the capacity for people to change. **You really can put things behind you and learn entirely new ways of seeing and feeling your world.**

The young man who started and stopped dozens of projects can learn to complete them and not self-sabotage by facing the anxiety he feels about whether he is capable. The woman who chose one unavailable partner after the other can finally learn to love a man of presence and depth if she faces her feelings of abandonment from her absent father. The mother who over-gives and compromises her health and body can get a personal trainer and therapist to reclaim her body if she faces her feelings of unworthiness for not being able to save her alcoholic mother.

In short, people can change when they can be the *Witness* to their own emotions and offer themselves compassion rather than criticism, in order to carve a path to courage.

If you look at the map of consciousness, you are actually bringing a higher frequency or feeling tone (power) to the part of you experiencing the lower frequency (force). This can happen between two people, such as during times when a wife offers acceptance to her husband around an issue he feels ashamed of, or when a psychotherapist offers empathy and compassion when a client reveals feelings or actions for which they criticize and shame themselves. Memory reconsolidation requires two things to occur: there must be a reactivation of the original feelings associated with the implicit memory, and there must be a mismatch to the original memory. The activation unlocks the old memory, and there is a window of opportunity during which a new and different experience can create change, thus the term "mismatch."

Do I really have the ability to choose?

The question of free will is a problem some philosophers have given up trying to solve, while others continue to tinker with it, and now scientists have presented new challenges. Relevant findings include the pioneering study by Benjamin Libet that show the brain activity related to a decision to move appears to begin briefly before people become conscious of it. We now know that at least some actions, such as moving a finger, are initiated unconsciously at first and enter consciousness afterward.

Similarly, we can develop a very powerful muscle of awareness when it comes to our emotions and reactions. To quote one of my heroes, Viktor Frankl, in the foreword of Stephen R. Covey's *Prisoners of Our Thoughts*, "Between stimulus and response there is a space. In that space is our power to choose our response. In our response lies our growth and our freedom."

"Between stimulus and response there is a space." *Zero Point* shows up again! To expand this space, you must strengthen your inner *Witness*, which you can do through meditation, prayer, and various forms of contemplation. In a 2007 study, Matthieu Ricard, a 66-year-old Tibetan monk who has meditated for years, was hooked up to 256 sensors for three hours, and the results showed that his brain produced gamma waves at levels that had never been reported in the neuroscience literature. Gamma waves are linked to consciousness, attention, learning, memory, and activity in the brain's left prefrontal cortex, which is associated with pleasant emotions and the capacity for happiness. Says Ricard, "Meditating is like lifting weights or exercising for the mind, anyone can be happy by simply training their brain."

When you choose to train unconscious habits and tendencies beforehand, you increase your capacity for free will. The ability to remain aware of yourself in the face of strong emotion is a skill that you develop over time. The *Path of Zero* is a path of courage to step into unknown territory. You just keep getting braver as you go, facing everything that arises along the way.

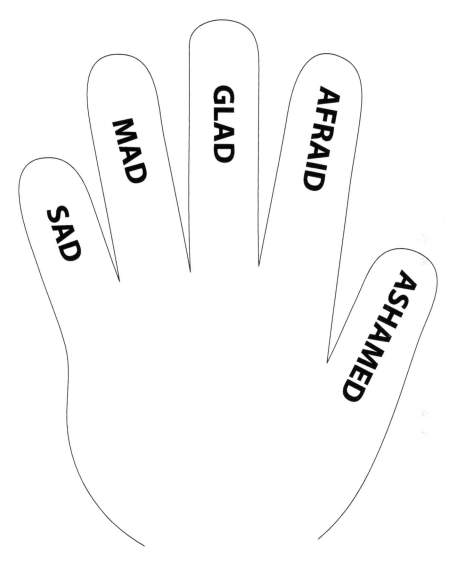

Think about it. You have all the ingredients right inside you to be a master of the *Path of Zero* if you can observe your emotions without judgment. When I work with people, I break it down into five main emotions. I have them hold up their hands and count them off: sad, mad, glad, afraid, ashamed. Although I have heard of other categories, in my experience, these five cover the range of emotion most people experience, and it has to do with degree beyond that. Sad can be melancholy or deeply grief-stricken, mad can be irritated or enraged, and so on. If you want to fine-tune your awareness, use Hawkins's map of consciousness, and whenever you feel a certain emotion, go for the next feeling up on the ladder. I keep a copy in my day planner so I can touch base with my intention if I feel wobbly. I always know I am heading for love.

If you are feeling guilt, apathy, or grief, see if you can move through fear and desire and reach for anger consciously—where you feel the anger of even having to deal with the issue. I personally use anger to fuel my transformation, and if I get stuck, it is in pride, which comes right before having the courage to see in a new way. I may linger in my own inflated sense of pride if I feel especially hurt, but eventually I feel the healthy pride of my own deservedness that says, "C'mon Kathleen, let it go. Just breathe and let it go. You know that's what love would do." The breath carries the intention to surrender into existence. I breathe one breath after the other into the center of my chest as the space around me becomes filled with breath and the intention to surrender. Somehow, as part of the Great Mystery, I get brave enough to let go. We can all develop that capacity, and the freedom is enormous when we do.

This *Path of Zero*, this movement of letting go, is both the movement of a single moment and the movement of a lifetime. It may be the path you take during an argument, when you drop your end of the rope and breathe into your heart, soften your belly, and begin to listen to the other person. It may be the path you take when you face the fact that you are no longer fulfilled in your job, or your marriage, or anything you had previously devised to keep yourself happy. It involves surrendering what you are experiencing and thus are identified with in order to open to something uncertain. It involves conscious suffering that you both experience and *Witness* within the larger context of your life. It involves a kind of spiritual or mystic death, after which you are changed, and life is no longer a dedication to self but a celebration of life. It involves showing up as who you really are.

Sometimes the very thing you have hidden, even from yourself, turns out to be the one precious thing about you that saves your soul. It is the place you refused to conform and go numb or be nice. When you face and surrender the emotions, especially the deep shame that has hidden this part of you, you begin to experience yourself as enough, and hope rises in the direction of your destiny.

A love story about the Path of Zero

To illustrate the essence of the *Path of Zero*, I would like to share with you of one of my favorite children's books, *Hope for the Flowers*—an allegorical novel by Trina Paulus first published in 1972 that reflects the idealism of the counterculture of those times. It is a story of taking the *Path of Zero* to experience a whole new life.

It is about two caterpillars, Yellow and Stripe, and their search for meaning. Stripe, the boy, began to feel restless, simply eating leaves and crawling on the ground. He thought there must be more to life than that and experienced the urge to ascend and be part of the sky. In his travels, he saw pillars in the distance reaching toward heaven and decided to boldly head in that direction. When he got to the base of one of the pillars, Stripe realized that the pillars were made up of struggling caterpillars like himself, stepping over one another to get to the very top. Before departing on his quest for the top, he met Yellow, a girl who also felt like there must be more to life than eating leaves and crawling on the ground and who also considered reaching the sky. But tender Yellow could not bear to step on other caterpillars to do that. Since they liked each other, they agreed to live together for a while.

Stripe's restless curiosity got the best of him, and he left Yellow to set off again for the tall pillars. He focused his intentions, and eventually he succeeded at reaching the very top of the pillar of weary caterpillars. From there, Stripe saw that there were countless other pillars filled with struggling caterpillars trying to get to the top of the heap, where there was nothing but lonely exhaustion from having to fight for the top. He was deeply disillusioned.

Meanwhile, Yellow answered the call to eat and eat until she spun a cocoon and hung upside down in the tree. Though not knowing where she was going, Yellow trusted the call and eventually emerged, transformed into a magnificent butterfly. She was able to soar effortlessly through the sky and had discovered the real answer to the feeling that there must be more to life than eating leaves. Now she was her true self.

As she effortlessly flew high, past the pillar of struggling caterpillars, Stripe saw this beautiful creature and recognized his beloved Yellow. She was a mirror to something in himself that he had forgotten and now had remembered. He climbed back down the pillar and when he reached the ground again, Yellow showed Stripe her empty cocoon, and he eventually realized what he needed to do. As Stripe spun a cocoon of his own, Yellow waited for him.

You can guess the rest of this story and it all started because Yellow made her life a large enough myth.

CHAPTER 6

Make Your Life a Large Enough Myth

*"If you are going to have a story,
you'd better have a big enough one or none at all."*
— Joseph Campbell

The great journey of your life

Let's face it, being human isn't easy. To believe in a bright future, whether for your own life or for the life of the planet, is a courageous act. This has been true at any time in history, but more so now than ever before.

For several chapters I have shared with you this notion of a *loveseed*. To anchor the main points, let's review what I have come to know to be true, and also where we are going. This is *my* version, coming from *my* *loveseed*, which is unique and is the center of my being and has some measure of ego or will attached to it, in order to impart this to you. It is personal to me, though I know that what I share with you has as much similarity as uniqueness for each of us, when it comes to our *loveseeds*.

For me, *loveseed* is a space of infinite potentiality. And it can be experienced by noticing how I feel in my body—noticing without judgment and with the understanding that I have buried my *loveseed* due to deep hurt at an earlier time in my life, often in childhood. I continue to keep it buried for fear of more hurt, yet that does not sit well with me, as I feel something is missing. My *loveseed* also contains the qualities of wisdom, courage, and love. I somehow know this and that I have this power within, yet I doubt myself. Others who have more fully developed those qualities of their *loveseeds* mirror back to me what is true about me that I cannot fully see, and I begin to feel more and more real.

I can go to this place, first, by witnessing my mind, then breathing into the center of my chest toward the back and being willing to let go of my thoughts, which is at times a sacrifice of many things, such as being right or better than, to hide the fact that I really doubt myself. When I keep my *loveseed* hidden, I feel inauthentic; not quite real.

This confuses me and the people in my life, who are also trying to sort this out. When I remember to surrender my mind, connect with my *loveseed*, and see the same in others, these challenges seem to diminish, and I feel joy. This whole movement to my *loveseed* and to all the other *loveseeds* is the great journey of my life that only I can take.

Picture this in your mind

What if you could see your entire life and all that has happened through the eyes of one who notices without judgment? What if you could see it all as one big *Path of Zero* after another—that is, as many journeys within a larger journey that has many dimensions, far more than you have considered thus far? The *Path of Zero* is the true hero/heroine's journey, where you learn to live at the center of your being rather in the layers of concepts and other adaptations that masquerade for the exquisite essence that is you.

I would like to show you some images that have helped my clients over the years. The first is this diagram, co-created with my colleague and friend Sherry Cupac. I have put this diagram on the whiteboard in my office for more than 25 years.

JOURNEY TO SELF

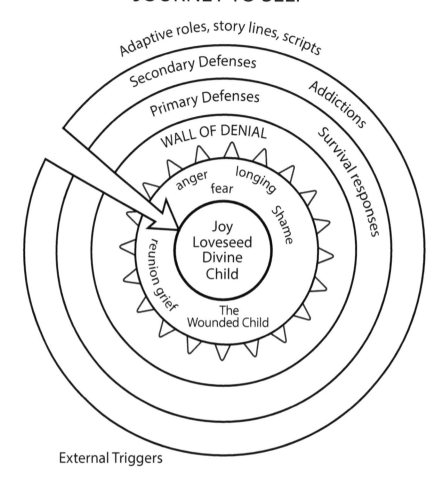

External Triggers

This is called The Journey to the Self, and in the center is what I call the *loveseed*. Think of it as your Divine Child essence. Directly around this essence is anger, shame, fear, longing, and even something called *reunion grief*. These are the emotions of the wounded child. As you get very close to what is true and real in yourself, the more pain can arise. If you really want something that feels missing for a long time, it becomes a painful subject. The longer you go without it, the more you begin to associate it with pain and deprivation. When you finally get something you've wanted for a long time, your anxiety goes up, because your psyche associates it with pain.

If you have the courage to let yourself feel the joy and love you have longed for, there is this kind of grief about all the time you lived without it. You did not allow yourself to feel that grief because it lived in your shadow—unconscious— as you did your best to cope. This is the *pain-body* that Eckhart Tolle speaks about when he describes this energy field of old, but still very-much-alive emotion, that lives in almost every human being.

We all learned to cope and adapt—some of us more than others, of course—and you can see in the diagram that there are primary and secondary defenses, survival responses, and addictions, as well as what we present to the world in our adaptive roles, storylines, and scripts. These are what Jung called the *persona*—the masks we present to the world. In early theater, the mask had a megaphone on it to make the sound louder. These are those "blaring" traits that others pick up on right away. Some examples may be the primary defense to be suspicious and guarded all the time, which can form certain lines upon the face to create a look of suspicion. This creates a vibration which then attracts things to fear. This may then manifest as the secondary defense of intellectualization, and, in fact, you may do well as a law professor or research scientist who does not deal with feelings and relationship drama, but with solving mysteries that then give a sense of control and security. There is nothing wrong with either of those professions, but perhaps you can see how these adaptations can cause a person to choose a course of study and a profession that is completely cut off from his or her true self, because the wall of denial prevents access.

When I worked in a psychiatric hospital, I encountered people who had figuratively and sometimes literally crashed into the wall of denial and had temporarily lost the ability to function in society. They came up against their depression or addiction or eating disorder over and over and had done all they could to avoid the deeper pain. For whatever reason, this time they could not hold up the defenses. They were more real than they had ever been. I was given the opportunity to show them their *loveseed*, and I knew that. I somehow realized the gift I had been given.

At one point, I was running seven psychodrama groups per week, carrying my big bag of scarves from unit to unit. Time and time again I watched people use imagination, play, and altruism to confront their demons, as those scarves served as everything from the habit of a nun to the scarf of a woman who always wanted to do a strip tease. It was the beginning of my career as a social worker and one of the most alive times of my life, because I was given the opportunity to see what was possible. I had them speaking with and embracing their disowned selves, which emerged in countless forms, creating new job descriptions for their addicted and depressed parts, and calling on God and in the form of

Shiva, Great White Buffalo, Kwan Yin, and Mother Mary. I wasn't thinking about the archetypal nature of it all, but living instead from that place.

I would guide each one of them to an encounter, and over and over again, I witnessed them experience sweet moments of recognition of their true selves; moments of communion they had longed for. Often, someone else in the group played the person's grandmother or a friend who showed unconditional love to them just as they were. Inside almost every person, there was this wise, loving being who emerged as they played the role for themselves, once it had been reflected by another. If it happened that the person's self-loathing was so great, someone else stood in that role for as long as it took, or they played it for another. They were naturally kind and helpful to each other, all being so broken, broken open, and so real.

There is always grief, and then joy, but if you don't understand that this is so, you could spend the rest of your life avoiding the very essence of who you are, thinking that the grief you are afraid of is all there is. You will find yourself repeating the same bad habit, getting into the same argument, or getting into the same dead-end job over and over again. In fact, to avoid the feelings of anxiety and reunion grief—and even anger that may arise right before the moment of reconnection—you may often unconsciously sabotage the very thing you say you want to do, such as write that book or lose that weight or commit to working in that career. Without an understanding of the powerful emotion of *reunion grief*, you could second-guess yourself, blame someone else for how you feel, or just shut down and numb out and disconnect from your *true north*, which is at the center of your being.

These emotions so prevalent in what Eckhart Tolle calls the "pain-body" in his visionary book, *The New Earth*—what we are calling reunion grief, shame, anxiety, and anger— are not just individual in nature. We are also tapped into and connected to the pain suffered by countless human beings throughout the history of humanity, which is a history of continuous tribal warfare, enslavement, pillage, rape, torture, and other forms of violence. This pain still lives in the collective psyche of humanity and accumulates on a daily basis, with insufficient attention paid to surrendering and releasing the pain. Just watch the news tonight or sit, as I do, with people as their lives unravel. The collective pain-body is encoded within every human's DNA, and each of us doing our part makes a difference for the whole.

The path is already there

Fortunately, there is something we can do about this pain. The arrow in the diagram below is the *Hero's Journey*, first described by Joseph Campbell his seminal text, *The Hero with a Thousand Faces*, otherwise known as the *Path of Zero*. You can consciously choose that path without first crashing into the Wall of Denial, but either way, you can make it a Hero's/Heroine's Journey. It's the difference between a story you would rather not tell and a myth that carries meaning for you and for humanity. Here's what it might look like:

The Hero's Journey

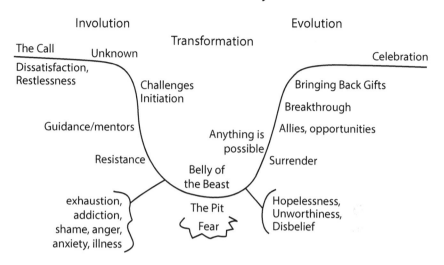

Looking at the *Hero's Journey* diagram, you can see that there are specific stages and challenges, where the protagonist must indeed slay dragons.

Imagine that. In each crisis; each challenge to our sensibilities, we have a powerful opportunity for opening. Most of us are not even aware that we keep our true potential at a distance by resisting our darker feelings. We may procrastinate on a deadline for fear of failure, which precludes the professional advancement we really want. We may ruin a romantic encounter by complaining so that we can pull away and not deal with our feelings of vulnerability. Even if life is stable and we feel content, we may pursue bits of chaos because we are not accustomed to feeling fulfilled and happy. Instead, we feel a restlessness; a kind of dissatisfaction with what is.

If we are lucky, something gets our attention along the way and there is a *call* to go downward/inward. It may first signal as depression, general malaise, or physical illness, but we find ourselves unable to go on. At the bottom of Diagram 2, you see the so-called "belly of the beast," a term that originally referred to the American prison system. Here you face the darker, more primitive aspects of your own nature; the parts of you hidden from the world as the result of prior neglect and/or abuse and imprisoned long ago by your own inner Judge. This is what Jung referred to as your *shadow*. In Volume 9 of *The Collected Works of C. G. Jung*, he writes, "The shadow is a moral problem that challenges the whole ego-personality, for no one can become conscious of the shadow without considerable moral effort. To become conscious of it involves recognizing the dark aspects of the personality as present and real. This act is the essential condition for any kind of self-knowledge."

The shadow is often associated with shame, and indeed, shame thrives in the shadow. In the shadow is also our "gold," our *loveseed*, that has been hidden. There are untold treasures within, and when you take the journey inward, you must face whatever is on the path as your own, the so called "good, the bad, and the ugly."

Considerable moral effort and the downward pull

What is this *moral effort* Jung speaks about? I believe that it is intimately connected to our *loveseed*, which is the source of the evolutionary impulse that even Darwin spoke about. His more widely-known first opus, *The Origin of the*

Species, focuses on genetic mutation and selection based on the survival of the fittest and seems to be a modern-day bible for the corporate and political world where, indeed, survival has to do with the biggest, the best and the most. This version is becoming extinct as his second and more mature work, *The Descent of Man*, shows how the foundational aspects of selectivity and survival are maintained, while a yet higher and more complex form of life evolves. This higher evolutionary cycle is fueled by the "higher agencies" of love and altruism, and the key is nurturance, an instinct that gives rise to and fosters love and altruism. Remember the *mirroring* and importance of having our *loveseeds* reflected.

Darwin's own observations indicated that natural selection promotes sympathy, social feeling, unselfishness, and even self-sacrifice. It recognizes no differences based on color, race, or any of the other differences humans express. He even argues that sympathy and social feeling most likely developed among less imposing and therefore "weaker" beings where affiliation was an advantage. This *sympathy* was actually what we refer to as empathy. According to *Johnson's Dictionary* (1755), sympathy is defined as a "fellow-feeling; mutual sensibility; the quality of being affected by the affections [feelings] of another."

Subsequent research shows that emotions and imagination play a major role in motivating us to develop a moral sense and actually help to form our *moral sense*. This moral sense is part of an evolutionary development that keeps us safe and thriving, and yet it is less and less valued and needed in our digitally-based world. The necessary feedback loop for us to continue to evolve is not happening. Play is happening on computers, often solo, and virtually, it is just as easy to blow someone up as it is to be kind. Nurturing, as needed by human beings and the Earth at this time, is simply being replaced by counterfeits of the original. We are connected horizontally through wireless devices, and yet not connected vertically to Spirit and at the deep level of our biology and our souls. **This creates a fierce downward pull on humanity; a sense of something important being missing, with its attendant feelings of insufficiency that lead to competition and greed, and it requires a fierce evolutionary impulse to change that course.**

In *The Heart-Mind Matrix*, Joseph Chilton Pearce makes the distinction between the *intellect*, which is a "head-based operation incorporating ever more complex variations and applications, each needing further explications and qualifications," from *intelligence*, "the automatic and natural state of the heart that brings coherence." He calls evolution the *transcendent* aspect of creation, which rises to go beyond itself, as life responds to its own ever-unfolding expression.

The power-tension of creative growth

There is a powerful tension to the creative process, as there is to the creative life—the life committed to going beyond the bounds and limitations of culture and consensus reality. There is also a powerful downward pull that begins to take hold when we move too quickly and are unable to be fully present to life and the feedback loop of present-moment experience. We have limbic systems and brains that require us to slow down enough to self-reflect and allow life itself to give us feedback. We neither "create" our reality, nor is it there as a pre-existing reality waiting for us to create within it. We are both creator and created, and our lives both create us and we create our lives either haphazardly like most people, or with a certain amount of intentionality.

Everything we encounter in life is being experienced on multiple levels or dimensions. Though there are many more dimensions and ways to categorize, the main ones we are concerned with here are the following:

- vibrational or energetic level (sound and light)
- physical or sensory level (body)
- emotional level (feelings)
- mental level (concepts, beliefs)
- mythic level (archetypal energies)
- spiritual level (transcendence)

Picture yourself as that big *Zero* in which it is all happening. **You are the space through which the Universe passes, and your story and the story of humanity are intricately interwoven.** You begin to know this at the mythic level, where you step into being a hero in your own life and become more aware of the story you are telling and how you are responsible for that story. It is your own, and yet, as you free yourself from the bondage of your own inauthenticity, you free others, because at the archetypal level we are all connected.

The force field of our myth

It is at this level that we can open to larger symbols in order to make connections and build bridges between the levels. **The myth we choose serves as a force field to illuminate the unfolding of our destiny.** Elizabeth Lesser says in *The Seeker's Guide*, "Viewing the contents of our minds and hearts as the work of archetypal forces depersonalizes much of our most human behavior. It counteracts the tendency we have to heap unnecessary blame on ourselves when we fail… OR… to get a thick head when we succeed."

It is important to remember that we are not meant to live as an archetype, but to identify with and make meaning of archetypal energies.

Returning to my client Jack, he had no adequate mirroring from either parent and now faces a challenge where he could potentially become heroic and go beyond the limitations of his own wounding, or not. He could make sure that his own children do not suffer that deep loss of inadequate parenting, or he could succumb to the survival instincts by which he has been driven his entire life and accuse their mother of adultery and attempt to bring her down. He could feel momentarily powerful, disown his own pain, and project it outward.

Since he had neither father nor mother as an example, he could tap into the archetypal realm to draw on the energies he needs to rebalance his life. The positive archetypal father figure is a strong male leader and has a distinct relationship with both the Shadow archetype and the Child archetype. This father must face his own Shadow so that he does not pass it on to his children. He undertakes the work of transformation in order to fulfill the role of Father and protect the Child.

In the history of humanity, we see examples of grounded, selfless, and strong father energy: St. Joseph; father of Jesus; Mufasa in *The Lion King*; God the Father; Gandalf from *The Lord of the Rings*, and countless others, each with their own unique flavor of father. There are also examples of shadow father energy where the battle within the man is expressed outwardly, often toward his own son. Darth Vader from *Star Wars* is a modern example.

Jack must now access this powerful, protective and loving energy inside himself, and in order to do so, he must pass through the layers of pain he has suppressed his entire life. He must surrender his attachment to the numbing effects of alcohol first, which is a huge task. He must be humble enough to receive the support he will need from allies who believe in his goodness.

There is a point of entelechy, or the point of connection, where one level is functionally you and the other is the Universe. It is the realization of the Soul of the Universe expressing itself through you. When you access this energy of archetypal dimensions consciously, you co-create your life in cooperation with the Universe.

Inside is the source of outside events. The way vibrational energy moves within the space of your body sets up the signal that attracts outside situations. **Your inner vibrational self, or loveseed, is the dominant site of change.**

It is very responsive and diaphanous to this Universal energy. This energy is the source of the evolutionary signal that is stirring up humankind at this time. Our "souls" are being stirred from within.

All energy moves from Source (vibrational) to the emotional body to the physical body. **We often attract a crisis to call on a mighty power within to go beyond a limitation.** We are vibrational beings and when we learn to energize ourselves from the inside via connection to our vibrational body (*loveseed*) rather than energizing ourselves from the outside via our connection to others, we claim a great power that can change everything, whether person, substance, or circumstance.

Understand this: **You are not separate from this energy.**

All the various ways we attempt to secure outside energy are subconsciously generated from the memory of how energy first came to us, which is our nurturing imprint. It is held as a deeply-ingrained limitation of energy flow arising from the imprint from your mother and father at birth.

Spiritual teacher Zoe Marae described it like this: "All life is like the river flowing. Mom is like the water in the river and the banks are like dad." (Translated, the feminine is the movement and the banks are the masculine structure.) "Without water, there is no river, and without the banks, there is no river." We need both masculine and feminine energies to flow. If Mom's river flows at 60 percent of her potential, and dad holds the banks at 40 percent of his potential, Mom carries more energy in this case, and thus more light. Most often, a child will identify with the parent with greater light, or take care of the one with less.

This imprint of our potential/ limitation is at the root of our yearnings, our connections, and our lives in general. **The limitation of this imprint dominates our entire reality until it is recognized. It is not necessary for this limitation to be repaired, but simply unselected by shifting and raising energy inside. Healing is experiencing and transcending— choosing a new story, a larger myth.**

The holy war inside

There are some people who naturally possess this inclination and are considered to carry the archetype of the Mystic. For most of humanity, it is the pain from our wounding that motivates us to make this journey or passage to deeper levels of our being where we access larger energies and greater possibilities. We must not let the scar tissue from the psychological level encapsulate us and keep us stuck in the layers, where we identify as broken or less than, and then settle for far less than our hearts long for. This is the mental level where you can confuse knowing for experiencing, and you will remain hungry just as if you ate the menu and not the meal. Much therapy happens here.

The ego is not concerned with flow but is held tightly on a grid of space and time and wants to make itself known and get it right. This is the unconscious downward pull in full force. We must transcend this need for control and reach for something much greater. In each of us there is a battle of the soul, or agony. *Agon* is a contest between two competing forces, archetypally-known as Light and Darkness. **We must pass through our own agony and not pass it on to someone else.**

There is this jihad, or holy war, inside each of us, between our own transcendent nature and the pull of darkness that manifests in our addictions and other forms of reactivity and compulsions. When we then experience guilt, even more resistance to flow is created. Guilt is a mental construct whose real energy is in the emotional realm. Mental guilt stays stuck in the system, blocking flow, whereas when we feel the feelings associated with guilt, energy returns to the system. Usually these are feelings of sadness and anger, often focused toward the self. We simply need to feel them.

We must bring radical compassion to the parts of us involved with those behaviors, and to any parts we have denied and even hated. The point of holy uncertainty where it no longer matters what others think of us is a point of grace. It is where we surrender who we have been and pivot to begin the ascent toward who we are becoming.

Darkness, descent, and conscious suffering

A door opens when we embody the knowing that we are fully responsible for our own darkness. Returning to Diagram 2, you can see that the Pit at the bottom is an inevitable aspect of this journey. It is essential that we begin with compassion and use it as a guide all along the way through darkness into the light, as a thread that connects us to hope—the kind of hope that David Steindl-Rast refers to in *Gratefulness, the Heart of Prayer* when he says, "The hope that is left after all your hopes are gone—that is pure hope, rooted in the heart."

The descent into unexplored aspects of the self is necessary on this journey, and we often must feel the pain inside the part of us that has been brutally victimized and neglected, by ourselves as well as others. **Self-compassion walks you through that door from victimhood into heart awareness.** It is the main quality needed to have the courage to ask the questions:

> Why do you *need* the darkness?
> What does it *provide* for you?
> What are you *afraid* of?

If you have read this far, you have felt the Divine restlessness that has you looking for more to become more. Just because you feel pain around it, and because it is difficult, doesn't mean you need to back off from this call. It is normal to remain loyal to your darkness, the limitations from your family, and even to your struggles and suffering, and there is a great resistance to letting it all go. If you walk on a path of awareness and intentionality, you can notice your resistance and not take any of it personally. Feel your frustration. Feel the pain of not fulfilling your potential. Let there be no judgment, but learn to walk the razor's edge, guided by compassion that comes from your Soul.

On the *Path of Zero*, you are meant to integrate all parts of yourself. No matter where you are and no matter what suffering you are still experiencing, see these symptoms as feedback on your journey of return. They are the natural pangs of birthing a new consciousness, which is a process of transmutation. We call this *conscious suffering.*

In *The New Earth,* Eckhart Tolle says, "Eventually suffering destroys the ego—but not until you suffer consciously. ... In the midst of conscious suffering, there is already a transmutation. The fire of suffering becomes the light of consciousness."

We suffer when our egos war on the path of integration with our higher self, and that is different from the *conscious suffering* required to pivot and truly transform. In the first case, we suffer because we feel the separation between our ideal self-image and where we presently are. In the case of *conscious suffering,* we feel the authentic pain of not being all we can be; of being separated from our *loveseed,* which is linked to *reunion grief.*

During a "dark night of the soul," which comes from the poem of the same name by Catholic mystic St. John of the Cross, the foreground of a person's existence seems to fall away, and he or she faces a kind of existential crisis. This crisis may be the dilemma of loving two people while married, of wanting to abandon a responsibility that would mean a total loss of identity, or of being caught doing something illegal. There is always the opportunity for great growth during these times, as we let go of the outer images of what we thought we were, to discover who we truly are.

Conscious suffering allows you to lead an epic life, where you are continuously offering your own suffering in service of others. There is a beautiful and ancient Tibetan

Buddhist meditation that spiritual teacher Pema Chodron teaches called Tonglen, which means "giving and taking." In this meditation, you deeply connect with your own personal pain and breathe consciously through the heart, and then do the same as you connect to all beings who suffer that same feeling of loss or betrayal or fear.

Our imperfections and our suffering bring us to our knees. If we are too perfect and cannot fail, we never surrender and cannot ever discover the true meaning of our larger purpose and realize the powerful quality of *amor fati*, a Latin phrase meaning "love of one's fate." It is used to describe an attitude in which everything in one's life, including suffering and loss, is necessary. We accept the necessity of it in the grand design of existence, simply because it is happening. **Amor fati means that you deeply accept the events and situations that have brought you to where you are.**

My client Tanya went through a bitterly-dark night of the soul as she discovered that Jeff, her husband of 28 years, had given her an STD. Jeff was a self-absorbed man who exhibited high ideals to their four grown sons and was a successful surgeon as well as the consummate family man who prided himself in how well he managed his perfect life. Attempts by Tanya to have a more meaningful relationship were met with defensive admonitions that she was not grateful for all he did.

After 28 years, the "house of cards" came tumbling down. Not only did Jeff sleep with another woman, but he flaunted it in Tanya's face and never acknowledged that he had hurt her. Rather, he justified his behavior based on how little he felt understood by her over all those years.

Believe me, *amor fati* does not happen right away. How could it? Tanya had to first feel the pain and anger of betrayal. Then, there was bargaining and the dance between the two of them that merely proved what she had known her entire marriage but had pushed away because it did not fit the narrative she held about marriage and family.

Fortunately, she reached out for help and began to move through the layers of emotion that had been buried and the feelings that arose as the divorce unfolded. She learned how to welcome whatever feelings arose and began to feel more alive long before the drawn-out divorce proceedings were complete. At one point, smiling across from me on my green couch, looking more radiant and younger than she had when I first met her, she declared the entire mess a blessing. She said that Jeff had done her a huge favor to be so consistently cruel that she could not second-guess her decision to leave him.

That was *amor fati*—not only the acceptance, but the celebration of what-was. The powerful energies of the archetype of Betrayal, which involves deception and broken trust, put an end to what needed to end a long time ago, and Tanya was grateful for the huge nudge.

I can honestly tell you that whatever predicaments your soul has gotten you into, you are in good hands. There are throngs of light beings rooting for you all the time.

You cannot do it alone

No one can control or be a match for their own darkness. To master the dark, you do not take out a sword, but rather you learn to be vulnerable, honest, and kind with yourself. You surrender, realizing that this part of you, this place you go, is something you must embrace. This entitled and downright nasty part of you is who you must come to know and love. Acceptance is a kind of passionate surrender, and the Universe is incapable of saying "no" to your intense yearning to be free. You must simply offer the Universe a passion equal to its own. There is no bribing the Universe, God, or whatever you call that power.

If you are not really up for the *conscious suffering*, I understand. Why, you may ask, would I want to suffer consciously? You don't need to. And returning to the caterpillar/butterfly story, you could remain a leaf-eating crawler your entire life and be happy with that. Maybe.

The work of ethnobiologist Elisabet Sahtouris provides an exquisite example of the process of transformation that is being asked of us on a global level today.

Sahtouris spent years studying the transformational process of caterpillar into butterfly, uncovering what she named imaginal cells. Because imaginal cells contain the DNA of the butterfly, which is slightly different from that of the caterpillar, the immune system of the latter views them as foreign objects and attempts to destroy them, the same way it would a virus or bacterium. In a similar way, humanity has done the same to our prophets, lightworkers, and truth-speakers.

However, there comes a time in the life of every caterpillar when they heed an innate call to begin a feeding frenzy, during which they devour everything in sight. During this time, the caterpillar basically dissolves into a nutrient soup, becoming a blob of goop. In the case of the caterpillar, the hyper-eating phase triggers a hyper-production of imaginal cells, which begin popping everywhere, and they gravitate toward each other, coalescing into imaginal clusters. Once the imaginal cells join together, the immune system of the caterpillar can no longer destroy them, no matter what it does. It tries and tries and fails and finally dissolves into a nutrient soup, a blob of goop, which is what the imaginal cells feed on as they transform into the butterfly.

In many ways, that is where humanity is now. Systems are imploding all around us; disintegrating in front of our eyes. What we thought we could put our faith in has failed us, and it is time to activate the innate design within each of us—and within the collective—to awaken to our full potential, refusing to live mediocre lives of frustration or to hide our light under a bushel.

No more excuses. We must find one another, and as we join in a deeper communion with one another, we can no longer be destroyed.

When we really begin to transform, within each of us there are parts of the old personality or ego that attempt to destroy what is being formed. We will get ideas or impulses or messages from our soul and then override them with fear-based thinking that calls us crazy or unrealistic.

Others who are afraid or jealous of your newfound self will attempt to knock you off track with their "helpful advice."

You get where I am going with this now. Let's face it: you have been a "blob of goop" like me a few times in your life. And whether you went through those events kicking and screaming or intentionally and with grace and ease, change happened.

In the new web of relationships based on love, kindness plays a huge role. We teach others how to treat us by how we treat them, which begins with how we treat ourselves. Yes, it all begins with you. It has to do with vows you have taken to fulfill a certain destiny in this lifetime. That is why so many of you are what I call "seekers," quite obsessed with knowing your purpose and how you can best fulfill a higher calling.

If you choose an epic life of transformation, it is because within an evolutionary context, you are wired to do so. Everything in your life is a mirror to help you correct course toward a brighter future, if you are willing to make that choice and move toward transcendence.

CHAPTER 7

Transcendence: Moving Through the Layers

"Take everything that's bright and beautiful in you and
introduce it to the shadow side of yourself... When you
are able to say, 'I am ... my shadow as well as my light,'
the shadow's power is put in service of the good."
– Parker Palmer

An end to the *Trance*

At this point you can see that the great anxiety
we feel (collective angst) is due to the disconnection
from our *loveseed*, which is Source. The great sadness
(collective grief) is what we feel when we finally get close
to reconnecting. The great anger (collective rage) is what
we feel when reconnection is thwarted. The great shame
(collective humiliation) is what we feel toward Self for
losing the connection to Source. The great joy we feel is

when we are reconnected. **The great danger to all of us is a humankind that is not connected.**

Imagine that all of life's drama is based on these five powerful emotions—sadness, fear, anger, joy, and shame—moving through you or not. What if my satisfaction and progress come from the movement of my emotions in my moment of experience rather than from outside achievement? It is this movement that fuels the *Hero's Journey*, which is always a descent into the darker, more primitive aspects of our nature, in order to connect to the real in us; to our *loveseed*. What if all of evolution is fueled by this impulse to return to the Source of our experience and then go beyond what we have known before? Transcendence. Trance-endence. The end of the *Trance*.

The triad of transcendence

There are different transcendent realms that allow for change in different ways:

Transformation is a very human way of change that involves shedding the old so the new can appear. We usually meet great resistance before this way of change is realized. The transcendent function is surrender.

Transmutation is the alchemical process of shifting a perception that releases the power to transcend. A hardship is experienced and the power of the hardship is released as the hardship is no longer needed when perception of the lesson is learned. Hardship is transformed to power through perception. The transcendent function is perception.

Transfiguration is the way of change that involves a metamorphosis of form. The actual physical is changed, as when there are spontaneous remissions of illness, or regeneration of limbs, as well as super-human strength when the situation calls for it. It is a kind of "magical" realm which is not entirely understood, and requires a humility and innocence that accepts that you know nothing, and are therefore open to infinite possibility. The transcendent function is innocence.

All of these ways of change access higher realms whose building blocks sing a very high note. The great obstacle to transcendence are the beliefs based on fear that we have accumulated in the course of our lives and in the grand unfoldment of humanity.

Time for a system upgrade

So much of the dysfunction we suffer in our lives is due to the split where people are literally cut off from the conscious experience of the emotions that arise in the body, and thus cut off from the body. Psychologist and emotional intelligence expert Daniel Goleman says that the human brain has not been upgrading its hardware as we've evolved, and we continue to have the same primitive reactions our ancient ancestors experienced that protected them against savage beasts. Learning to tame the reptile inside is one of the things I do most often with clients.

The amygdala is the center of the brain that controls the survival response, and also recognizes emotions and allows us to attune to others. What a choice we have in every moment! We can become a snake motivated by pure instinct, or a bodhisattva motivated by compassion. When threatened, the amygdala can respond irrationally and destructively. Goleman calls this an *amygdala hijack,* which diminishes our performance, our abilities, and our capacity for connection. It erodes our self-esteem by continuing to have our best-self hijacked by our inner serpent.

If you have ever found yourself startled by something that looks like a snake and then quickly recover from the startle as you realize the thing is a stick, you averted an amygdala hijack. You know you have had an amygdala hijack if you have a sudden onset of strong emotion, after which, upon reflection, you realize you acted inappropriately, or are completely confused. You may have screamed or thrown something, or expressed your emotions by blaming others or yourself. Regardless, your brain is reacting to a past memory, because your amygdala has found a match in the trigger of the present moment.

If the amygdala does not find any match to the stimulus received, then it acts according to the directions received from the neo-cortex—the more evolved part of the brain. Without the emotional charge, a hijack is averted. In *Breaking the Habit of Being Yourself,* Spiritual teacher Joe Dispenza says, "A memory without the emotional charge is called wisdom."

To avoid a stressful life of continuous amygdala hijacks or the fear of them, you need to develop what Goleman calls *emotional intelligence* and build the muscle of choice through practice, upon which you can build spiritual intelligence. This is the system upgrade he speaks about. Observing your world from a firm standpoint of the *Witness*, you must surrender getting attached to each strong emotion as it arises, knowing that nothing is personal. This is the *Path of Zero*, where you consciously breathe into your heart and expand your awareness to allow whatever you are feeling to be there. If you can remember to ask "What would love do?" you are becoming a master.

We now understand that our experiences are produced by the underlying structures and processes of the brain, which then affect the mind and thus, the emotions. The mind depends on the brain, and as the brain develops in childhood, so does the mind. Damage to the brain leads to damage to the mind. Mental activity maps to neural activity. Co-authors of *Buddha's Brain*, Richard Mendius and Rick Hansen write, "Apart from potential transcendental factors, the brain is the necessary and proximally-sufficient condition for the mind; it's only *proximally* sufficient because the brain is nested in a larger network of biological and cultural causes and conditions, and is affected itself by the mind."

Here we have another example of a strange loop that is not completely understood as yet: how the brain makes the mind or how the mind uses the brain to make the mind. What we do know is that as your mind awakens, so does your brain, so if you are at all interested in enlightenment or living a truly fulfilled life, training your brain is key.

The human nervous system has been evolving for 600 million years, and our ancestors, who needed to be very aware of dangers, losses, and conflicts, passed on their genes to us. In order to survive, their brains evolved a negativity bias that looks for danger and bad news, reacts intensely to it, and then stores that information in neural structures. A key to this negativity bias is the power that the emotion of fear has over us. It is not uncommon for people to overestimate threats and underestimate opportunities and support. **Negative experiences sensitize the brain to the negative, which is why negativity breeds negativity, and it is common for people to spiral down from the pull of negativity in their environment.**

The negativity bias may be good for survival in harsh conditions, but it is a really big obstacle to quality of life, fulfilling relationships, personal growth, and health. Strengths such as optimism and resilience come mainly from positive experiences. Ironically, unless we pay mindful, sustained attention to them, most positive experiences do not have a lasting impact on us. They may be momentarily pleasant, but in terms of changing neural structures, they just don't have the impact of the negative. It's as if the brain is like Velcro when it comes to negativity and like Teflon when it comes to positivity.

Gratitude is one of the most potent balms to the negatively-biased brain. It helps us to loop back and transform the instinct of fear into the evolutionary impulse from our *loveseed*. It helps us to release the fear, because if we can feel gratitude, we still have what is important.

In *Women, Food and God*, Geneen Roth writes, "Imagine knowing that nothing will destroy you. That you are beyond any feeling, any state. Bigger than. Vaster than. That there is no reason to use drugs because anything a drug could do would pale in comparison to knowing who you are. To what you can understand, live, be, just by being with what presents itself to you in the form of the feelings you have."

It is good for us to imagine such a life and to imagine such a world, because the more we imagine that, the more we lean away from fear toward love.

Emotions as source energy

Emotions are physiological states or processes and reactions that happen in the body. Feelings are the subjective experience of our emotional states. They are more experiential and provide a bridge to thought, as in, "I feel afraid." They are not the fear, but the feelings about the fear. Feelings and emotions are often used interchangeably, and they are very close.

When I help couples deal with conflict and I ask one person to tell their partner how they feel as a result of the current issue, I usually get something like this: "I feel that you were unfair, and that you didn't consider me in what you were doing," which does not describe a feeling at all, but rather, a judgment and a story—both mental processes. I then hold up my hand and say, "sad, mad, glad, afraid, ashamed," and the truth comes out. "I felt sad and afraid," or "I felt mad and sad." Their partner is suddenly able to connect, to relate, as the feelings easily resonate within the limbic systems of the two of them.

Thoughts are the mental labels, categories, and concepts with which we organize our experiences. We automatically label an emotion or feeling experience and store it somewhere in our mind. The stronger your experience of emotions and feelings, the more vivid your thoughts will be and thus the more space the emotions will take up in your short- and long-term memory, which then leads to the creation of beliefs. For many people, this then becomes their identity.

When we experience intense emotions and feelings as a result of our parents' (or any important authority figure) disowning their emotions and feelings, we end up with the dysfunctional loop of *carried emotions*. Dad experiences shame below the level of awareness when he sees his adolescent daughter dressing in a provocative manner, but he expresses it as anger. The daughter then experiences the shame, which is not her own. She may repress and deny it and lash out in anger or turn it toward herself. When working with an adolescent girl whose father shamed her for her developing breasts, the self-loathing she experienced was so intolerable that she began cutting her inner thighs to draw blood and thus to externalize her pain. As parents, doing the work of owning our own shame is one of the most important tasks we face.

Emotions need to move and flow, and if they do not, there is a failure to complete the loop of awareness from emotions to feelings to thought, which can lead to emotional reactivity. When emotions flow like a river, there is no identity, as in the *Path of Zero*, and thus no need to react.

Emotions are vibrational and the body is physical. As long as the emotions flow, endless vitality is created in the body. In a spoken teaching, Zoe Marae said, "Emotions are units of movement. When you experience an emotion, a movement of vibration is created which generates vitality and health. Denying or controlling an emotion stops the movement of vibration which generates exhaustion and physical decline."

Emotions arise when you are affected by the experiences that you have attracted by your inner signal. As soon as you make emotions psychological with your concepts from the mental body, there is confusion. They are simply sensations that rise up when you are touched by something, and you don't need to take them personally. They are meant to flow through you with ease, opening you up to your connection to the vibrational body, which is connected to Source, which is your *loveseed*, and which gives you more energy. As your energy or vibration is raised, what you attract on the outside is raised up as well, and you begin to find that reflected in greater health, wealth, and nourishing relationships.

Attempts to hold back and control your emotions causes you to lose power, because you don't connect with—and take feedback from—the moment of your experience. The movement stops and the energy drops. In the case of dis-ease, unfinished emotions from the past block emotions from flowing, and thus the connection to the vibrational body or Source is lost. A part of the physical body is left alone, disconnected from Source, and must generate energy on its own. The body reacts by creating inflammation around the part that is cut off from Source.

This unfinished emotional blockage is actually what you need to pay attention to. It is trying to get your attention by coming up over and over until you deal with it. You need to feel it to heal it. It doesn't matter whether you feel positive or negative emotions, for they both give rise to inner vibrational energy. You will have more resistance when you judge something as negative, so keeping your judgment out of the equation is essential. You must make room for all emotion; all experience. You must cultivate an attitude of having no preference toward all emotion, which frees you from the tyranny of opinion.

Interrupting rewind

The pineal gland is located within an area of the brain known by the Taoists as the Crystal Place. This area consists of the pituitary gland, hypothalamus, thalamus, and pineal gland. When these glands are functioning properly, chemicals are produced that expand our consciousness and can evolve humanity into alternate worlds that lie beyond this third-dimensional reality. Humanity has attempted to stimulate this area of the brain with hallucinogenic and divinatory plants for thousands, if not millions, of years. As a result of the ongoing expansion of consciousness, the accumulated energy has created a vortex of increasingly high-vibrational energy that is mirrored in what many call the Ascension Process, or the New Earth. Change is on all levels on the Earth herself and within each of us, her children.

Belief systems based on the emotional output of fear shut down the production of these major chemicals, which are amino acids that were once produced in the womb and in infancy until the age of 12. Calcification occurs within the pineal gland after the onset of puberty, which sets the body into a decline toward death, and the body is placed on a timer. It is as if we are a fully-charged battery at birth, gradually losing energy over a period of time, if you buy into the illusion of consensus reality. When you connect to your *loveseed*, the battery does not run out.

Comparable to the calcification that occurs in the pineal gland, our perceptions become solidified and we no longer look past the horizon of our limited vision. This happens more out of an acclimatization to the high-stress norms of the prevailing culture. Like the frog in cold water that doesn't know it's slowly being cooked as the heat is turned up, when we are run by fear, we fall into the *Trance*, all the while in rapid decline.

As previously noted, fear-induced emotions such as depression, anger, and worry cause the body to develop an addiction to the chemical being produced. When we add to these emotions beliefs such as "I am a loser," "I am not worthy," "I have been ripped off," a powerful *trance* state is induced. Emotions are magnetic, and thoughts/beliefs are electric. When we wrap a thought or belief around an emotion, an electromagnetic charge is formed that keeps us stuck in the matrix of our own making. That is what ages us far more than the natural physical decline that comes with age. This unconscious YES to the charged negative belief sets off a cascade of chemical reactions that create dis-ease.

Candace Pert, one of the most respected researchers in the area of mindbody medicine, has proven in her groundbreaking work *The Molecules of Emotion* that the very same chemicals that run our body and brain are the chemicals that are involved in emotion. If we want to take better care of our health, we cannot pretend that emotions are not a key player.

We would not have been created with the magnificent capacity to feel our emotions (energy in motion) if it was not part of the Divine Plan. Without them, we could not bond with the people we love, we could not feel inspired to create magnificent art and music, and we could not feel the joy that is our birthright. We must, however, align our capacity to feel with our sovereign will.

Each one of us is a unique multidimensional being on a cosmic mission. Our primary purpose, before all others, is to awaken from the slumber that being born into the third-dimensional matrix has created. It is imperative that we dissolve the past or at very least shift away from the pattern of rewind, where we keep going back in an endless loop at a superficial level. If we do not, our ability to use our emotions as the doorway to higher consciousness will be virtually impossible. We will constantly recycle the memories of the past and create our lives from the old models.

As fearful stuff comes up, we are faced with two choices: grab hold and argue for your limitations and recycle, or let it go, which may mean leaving the marriage, leaving the job, letting go of the anger, letting go of the blaming, and so on. To do this, we must radically shift our perceptions, which means radically shifting our emotions, since emotions are the vehicle of perception. **In a very real sense, our higher emotions are like an upgraded organ of perception that we must hone in order to evolve.**

Everyone is subject to the downward pull exerting an influence. While you live your life believing one thing, a deeply-held unconscious belief can begin to manifest. As you learned in the previous chapter, this belief begins to take hold as a *shadow* energy, often distorting the natural impulse to make sure that all are cared for, including one's self. In its place arises the inner pressure of the survival part of the brain, creating an intensely-felt need to accomplish one thing to get to another and another on the trajectory of endless oversized goals, so that the weary person can finally feel successful. There is no experiencing of the moment, and the inner signal is one of fear.

This drive can bring people to their knees and is often confused for ambition. **There is a vast distinction between ambition of the ego and that of the soul. One is out for self alone, while the other is out for the common good.**

In a sense, the *Hero's Journey* is a descent into our darker, more primitive nature to complete a loop—to integrate this "shadow." Even as we have entered this brave new world of instantaneous global communication, for most people the lines of communication between who we think we are and what we feel deeply in our bones are sadly broken. And no, there is no pill that can "cure" that chasm. There is only awareness, love, and the miracle of transformation and integration.

There is simply no shortcut. If you intend to be a co-creator of a better world for you and for others, you must not be afraid of your shadow, and you must undertake the work of transforming yourself. Mystics and poets understood these things without the need for proof, because they listened to the pulse of the Universe inside themselves. Rumi says, "Yesterday I was clever, so I wanted to change the world. Today I am wise, so I am changing myself."

What is the shadow, really?

Our paths are carved by the most inconspicuous thoughts, often never discovered. Every human being carries a shadow, and the less awareness we have of this part of us, the more powerful and more dense it is, exerting its wobbling affect in all we do, until we find ourselves completely off course.

Not only are there individual shadows, we must contend with familial, cultural and collective shadows, as well. These occur when we project onto a group of people qualities and attributes that are disowned or repressed in the society at large. The United States has a huge sexual shadow, as we have not fully integrated Puritanism with the hedonistic yearnings that become stronger the more they are repressed. The deep, dark shadow of slavery that was not fully integrated during the civil rights movement continues to rear its head in the racial tension that plagues the "land of the free" today.

Partial integration does not work but reinforces the repression when we believe we are "over it." We don't get over our shadow or grow out of our shadow, but must learn to integrate it fully, which often means doing a great deal of reparation for the damage it has caused, as anyone who has ever done the Steps in AA can attest to. Often the amends are more to the Self.

We must then incorporate the shadow into the other aspects of who we are, which entirely transforms who we thought we were. Something new is created out of the darkness. Due to the way we are wired and have developed, no one avoids having a shadow, so beware the person who plays the saint. The shadow is most often associated with darkness, fear, and danger, and yet that is simply a cultural myth, for there can also be power and goodness in the shadow, and goodness comes from facing one's shadow.

The shadow contains what we perceive to be our negative traits—negative aspects of self we don't like, the parts that aren't so pretty or acceptable, or aspects of self we may hold in disdain or even contempt. In some circles it is called the lower self. Encounter with the shadow is often described in metaphors such as facing our demons, slaying the dragon, dark night of the soul, or the more common, midlife crisis. Addictions develop as we medicate the perceived pain of the encounter, and the "nervous breakdown" happens when we refuse the encounter.

As you can see, burying the *loveseed* is closely related to the development of the shadow in childhood, where we learn to put away parts of ourselves that were not valued by our family or culture. As we bury those parts of us, we also bury the emotions associated with the lack of acceptance or devaluation. This leads us to bury the shame and feelings of worthlessness with the shadow, as well as the anger at losing a part of self. We were not taught how to live with and embrace these vulnerable emotions, and the longer we ignore them, the stronger these exiled parts of us become. The greater the wounding and trauma, the more split off; the more buried. As Robert Bly says in *A Little Book on The Human Shadow,* "Every part of our personality that we do not love will become hostile to us."

Bly describes the average one- or two-year-old child as having a 360-degree personality, from which energy radiates out from all parts of the body and the soul of the child. The child running and screaming for joy is a ball of energy, and when a parent says things like, "You need to be quiet and still," or, "Share with your sister," the child puts the exuberant or greedy part of the self in an invisible bag that she or he then carries around in order to be acceptable. By the time the child gets to high school, peers are the ones determining which parts need to get stuffed into the bag, and the entire first 20-25 years of a person's life are spent filling that bag with precious aspects of the Self, thus burying the *loveseed.*

If you don't want to be hunched over by midlife, it's wise to begin unpacking that bag—and if you are really going for the gusto of who you are, get well-acquainted with and even devour the contents of the bag, which is Bly's way of describing the integration of the shadow.

Amidst the shadow, there are gifts, as well. Creativity is often lurking in the shadow, but if you grew up in a family that valued logic and intellectualization, that juicy part of you can get hidden for a lifetime.

One of my clients, Louise—who suffered from ADD and bipolar disorder and on medication for more than 40 years—struggled to feel her emotions in a way that did not send her to bed for days. She was either totally out of touch, or "going down the rabbit hole," as the saying goes. For weeks at a time she got snagged into endless negative loops that prevented her from doing anything productive.

She had a PhD in psychology, but never passed the licensing exam due to the disorganization of her thinking under stress and the effects of ADD. She had an ocean of shame inside that she kept at bay for years, but which began to break through in the course of our work together. She seemed to make progress, but would quickly slide back, as she continued to be overtaken by beliefs that always led to self-loathing or blaming those close to her. The integration process was at a standstill.

When I suggested Louise begin painting, miracles began to happen. For one, she unleashed her creativity and found she had quite a flair for abstract painting. Her art is filled with emotion and movement, which she was unable to achieve internally. Each time she created a painting, she unleashed energy, thereby reorganizing her inner landscape. Her primary focus was to have self-compassion, and as she did that more and more often, the conflict in her marriage lessened.

Shadow work is bringing to consciousness that which has been hidden, rejected, and disowned. The shadow thrives in the dark where no one can see. Often as someone struggles with an affliction or addiction—whether it be pulling out one's hair to self-soothe or even the darker expressions such as alcoholism and drug addiction or watching child pornography—the habit intensifies as the person is too ashamed to ask for help. Bringing the shadow out of darkness and into the light of consciousness in a spirit of compassion, acceptance, and curiosity is what begins to integrate the shadow.

Why must we work with the shadow?

The most important reason for you to do your shadow work is that you cannot fully experience the wholeness of who you are without putting your arms around the exiled parts of you and bringing them "home" to yourself. Integrally connected to that is the fact that in order to be healthy physically, emotionally, and spiritually, you need the energy that is tied up in your shadow.

If you have a long-empowered shadow, it will naturally take more energy to suppress it, which means less energy available for living. Jung believed that what is repressed in the unconscious comes to us as fate, where some unknown part of us leads us to our destiny. As you can see, it's a very good idea to harness the power of your shadow in the direction you want to go, rather than letting an unknown sub-personality take the helm of your life's ship.

The more you believe in your own goodness and wholeness, the more easily you can work with the shadow without destroying your healthy ego. When I work with couples, they often present as blaming the other, which tells me they have not yet faced and integrated their own shadow energy, and still see it in the other. It is so unconscious that one will criticize the other for being critical; calling the other names for having been called names. The childlike immaturity is so blatant and yet neither can see it due to their emotional blindspots.

Being nonjudgmental is the key to shadow work and then eventually bringing in compassion. These often nasty parts of us must be seen as long-lost children who need to be loved. Tara Brach, a Buddhist teacher and author of the book *Radical Acceptance* says, "Clearly recognizing what is happening inside us, and regarding what we see with an open, kind and loving heart, is what I call Radical Acceptance."

This is active work. Whatever arises in your exploration of your shadow has value and growth for your development. As the Buddhist nun and spiritual teacher Pema Chodron says in *When Things Fall Apart*, "Nothing ever goes away until it teaches us what we need to know."

The shadow is most often very well defended. One way we can begin to know our shadow is to notice what we judge intensely. Who and what about them do we judge? There is a tendency to project our disowned "stuff" outward.

When we do the work of integrating our shadow, our rage transforms into power, our terror transforms into excitement, and deep grief transforms into compassion. Always, at the bottom of everything, there is love.

Looping back to integrate the shadow

Shadow work is the heros's journey we spoke about earlier, and is the metaphor for the creative process of integrating our darkness to live an authentic life. There are three main steps to the mythic pattern of the hero or heroine, which is a journey of looping back to discover and embrace lost parts of the self. It is also called the path of return, because you are returning to your true nature.

1. **Separation**—There is a turning toward the self, a descent away from the outer world into the place inside where life is inspired and into the depths where feelings live. Separation has the symbolic echo of a baby being separated from the mother and so has a scary feel to it. I find that most people resist this in a big way.

2. **Initiation**—The hero or heroine is initiated into true heroic stature by various rituals and rites; daring and battle. Through that which is not authentic falling away, the true character emerges—*the loveseed.* Full-blown initiatory experience is when you have no control, can't pick the rules, the rules change, and you have to play the game, regardless.

3. **Recognition**—The hero or heroine returns in triumph to the well-earned recognition, although this in itself has its own trials and tribulations.

On the path of return, all our addictions and afflictions are seen as birth pangs of a new consciousness, where we must become both the shepherd and the lamb we have lost in our quest for survival. The lamb is our gift, and on the path of return, as was written in Isaiah 11:6, "The wolf will live with the lamb, the leopard will lie down with the goat, the calf and the lion and the yearling together; and a little child will lead them." In this statement, this peace-filled condition was referring to the *peaceableness* of the Messiah's kingdom. It is a place within each of us that knows the infinite; where the heart and mind, the compassionate brain and the survival brain, and the masculine and feminine energies all work together in the infinite loop of life. This is heaven on Earth. All of us on Earth belong to heaven, and heaven belongs to us as we emanate as love itself.

CHAPTER 8

Love Itself

"Love isn't something you find.
Love is something that finds you."
— Loretta Young

Disintegration in the service of integration

We are being asked to evolve to a higher order of harmony, and in the process, we often disassemble our lives through crisis. We must remember that this disintegration is in the service of transformation into a higher order of integration. and it is up to us to decide the higher meaning of our suffering.

Suffering stems from the gap between who we think we are and who we really are. This is the wound; the pain-body; the black hole that devours our energy and leads us to repeat the same unmerciful acts over and over.

The integration involves a journey to the repressed depths of one's psyche, where the raw truth of our experience is felt. This descent is considered a feminine model of transformation toward wholeness and is essentially the task of giving birth to one's true Self. Women more often experience the pain of inner dissonance as their feminine nature is not supported by the culture at large, and they attempt to fit into a masculine model of success, creating imbalance.

Now more than ever I see that the masculine model of wholeness is no longer adequate, and more and more, men are forced to relate differently to their own depths if they are not to be swallowed by depression or addiction, both symptoms of not facing the deep, dark feminine. Men, too, must have the courage to dare the descents that permit them to reclaim the instinctual and wounded parts of themselves and to become capable of real relationship.

The call

My own story of "falling from grace," which has led me to live more fully from the *loveseed* within me, was the backdrop for a wondrous adventure where I came face to face with my own fear, hidden in my shadow–the part of me I had not yet learned to love. So much of who I am today was buried along with the fear, which my own heroine's journey uncovered.

Every hero's or heroine's journey begins with a call to wholeness, although that truth is not always in conscious awareness for quite some time. I had already taken courageous steps in the direction of my own liberation when I closed my thriving psychotherapy practice and moved to Cusco, Peru, for 11 months in 2005. It was a sudden move, spurred by the unexpected death of my young cat Haley, named after Haley's comet. This small creature had burst onto the scene of my life, as her name implies, and landed right in my heart, then died quickly from an unknown illness. In a mere three months, my entire world was turned upside down as the grief burst me open to possibilities I had never imagined before. At that point in my life, my children were grown and I was single, and I actually had the time to fully feel my grief and loss.

Prior to Haley's appearance, I was happy and content with more clients than I could keep up with, and I was healthy, fit, and in a training program to become an executive coach. Though I felt professionally accomplished, I had this feeling that there must be something more and imagined that working with a different clientele would bring the change I wanted. I loved my work with couples, but I was single and had been for a while, and there was far too often an ache in my heart alongside the joy when I helped a couple drop their defenses and step into a space of empathy and acceptance. My divorce and then the end of another very important relationship had taken years to grieve fully, and Haley had opened my heart again, in a most innocent way. When she died, I felt bereft.

Fully feeling the grief over Haley connected me to all my other losses, to my reunion grief, and to the realization of how I held myself back my entire life, always tending to the needs of others. It was the fully-alive Kathleen whom I really missed, and the joy I felt with Haley prompted that part of me to surface again. Never underestimate the influence a furry four-legged friend can have in your life!

One day, after walking into my newly-painted living room—a superficial attempt to take the knife out of my heart—I heard a voice say, "You will be moving. Don't paint anymore." The voice came from inside, and very quickly I realized that it would be a big move. The energy released by surrendering to the grief over losing Haley infused me with a new level of intuition and courage. I said YES and decided to take a year off, without knowing where I would go.

To begin the journey, a heroine (I will use the feminine version, but this applies to heroes as well) must be called away from the ordinary world. This does not always mean she must literally move from her home and family, but in my case, it meant just that. "Called away" has many forms. It could be to enter the world of dealing with cancer or moving to a new line of work. There must be a kind of separation from the everyday world. It is usually a discovery, an event, or some danger that starts the heroine on her path. Most heroines have some reluctance to accept the call at first, but in the end, all heroines accept their destiny. Some happen upon their quest as if by accident, which the tarot card *The Fool* indicates. It involves *amor fati* and is part of being a heroine.

In *Hero with a Thousand Faces*, Campbell describes the new world the heroine enters as a "fateful region of both treasure and danger." I was soon to discover how true this is.

172

People asked me where I was going, but I had no clear answer for several months. Somehow, as never before, I trusted I would know. The choice to move to Peru was as synchronistic as everything else in my life at that time. When my friend Heather suggested Cusco, I had a feeling of YES, though I did not even know where it was. In an online search for "Cusco" I felt my heart open as I read about this magical city high in the Andes. Soon I was off on a great adventure! I immediately put my townhouse on the market, found someone to take my other cat, and began the process of closing down my practice, which would take several months, yet my great adventure had already begun.

The deeper meaning

On December 26, 2004, a deadly tsunami devastated Southeast Asia, and the mind of the world was riveted. What I witnessed is how the heart of the world grieved together, as we do when global disasters occur in this age of instant media. I witnessed couples who had previously been bitter and acrimonious cling to each other. One of my crankiest and most complaining clients had become so grateful for everything in his life, including the job he hated. A wave of compassion swept over the planet, and it was not only palpable, but measurable. I witnessed the same after September 11, but it was not as pure, because there was fear as well.

I decided that while I was in Peru I would allow myself the great gift of fully experiencing whatever would teach me about being compassionate and help me surrender the anxiety about not enough time, which had tyrannized me my entire life. I wanted a new relationship with myself and with time itself.

I was vigilant during the months prior to leaving about the naysayers, the people who either directly or implicitly judged me as crazy for doing what I was doing. Others viewed me as brave. I was crazy-brave. I knew it and I was good with that. I was 53, and frankly, I had reached the point in my life where it did not matter much what others thought. This quality alone is one of the biggest benefits of aging.

My plan was to fly to Cusco on February 4, 2005, and there was so much to prepare.

I was learning to trust a new voice, which I had listened to before, when I left my marriage. It was stronger now, and I knew it was the voice of my soul. I was following my bliss.

The navel of the world

I knew little about my new home, and I knew no one there. My Spanish was inadequate to be sure, but I had courage and a dream in my heart. I cried out of utter joy the first day I arrived in Cusco and sat on a balcony over the lively main square. I watched as the other-worldly glow of late afternoon light began to fade in the shadow of the majestic mountains surrounding Cusco; the city known as "the navel of the world."

For the next three days after that beautiful moment, I writhed in pain, alone in a bed and breakfast room. I had a high fever and couldn't eat. I was barely able to get to the toilet. I was delirious much of the time, like when I was a kid, feeling as if bugs were all over me. I had this *Witness* to the whole situation, and on the third day I became a bit concerned that maybe I was in trouble, not because of the bugs, but because I was dehydrated. I tried to call for help on the second day, but I was too weak. Late that evening, the owner checked in on me and brought me coca leaf tea to help me acclimate. I began to come around later that day and joined the other travelers for breakfast on the fourth day. Hello Cusco!

There is much to share about living in Peru, and I will share the highlights, yet continue on with the story of becoming lost, for it is as important if not more important than the story of being found. I opened myself to countless magical experiences and opportunities to shed my layers and outer identities. I was simply a woman living in Peru. I was not in the role of mother, therapist or guide of any sort. For the first time in my life I slept as much as I wanted, read whatever I desired, and discovered my own unique rhythm to daily life.

The trip to Tipon

Because I was alone so much of the time, I reflected and wrote and my inner poet came alive as she had been at previous times in my life, usually when I was deeply depressed or in love. This time, I felt more grounded and at the same time more in touch with my spiritual nature than ever before. I visited the ruins and took myself on excursions to sacred sites, inspired by the moment. On this particular Sunday, after living in Cusco for a month, I took a local bus to the town of Tipon, where an intact ritual garden of the Incas had survived, with elaborate water channels and archeological wonders. It was hilly and strenuous, and I loved being on the land and learning about the history. I recall looking down over the valley and fully realizing what a gift I had given myself. I was filled with gratitude. And I felt at home.

I preferred to travel on the local buses for the pungent taste of local life it provided. I wanted to feel a part of and not apart from everything. After Tipon, I ate cuy, which is baked guinea pig, because that is what they did on Sunday in the town I was in. On my return from Tipon to Cusco, the bus was filled with people dressed in their Sunday-best on the way to visit family for dinner.

I sat near two Indigenous women with long black braids, whose skin next to mine was many shades darker. A Mestizo woman sat across from me, darker than I, yet lighter than the woman next to me. I was so aware of all the shades and wondered what they felt toward me. My heart was open after a day of adventure, and I felt warmth toward everyone.

As the bus stopped, a man with a baby about six months old and an eight-year-old boy stepped onto the bus. The man looked at the woman next to me and handed the baby to her, each with a kind look toward the other, and not a word. We were at the front of the bus, and they went to the back where there was standing room only. For the next 20 minutes, the woman so lovingly cared for the baby, and all four of us women were drawn together by the experience, which transcended all differences.

At a later stop, the man and the boy came to the front of the bus, and without a word other than the man thanking the woman, the woman lifted the baby to the man, who then got off the bus with the young boy. I wondered what had just happened, and then I got it. This was the way they shared the responsibility of children. It was that safe for the man to pass his child to this woman he did not know. I felt so touched and amazed. I wondered what had happened in the United States. The war in Iraq was raging, and things were less and less safe in every way. I was so sad for my country, and sobbed all the way home. About that day, I later wrote this poem:

SUNDAY

There are still places
where people care that it is Sunday
and wear fancier clothes
to visit friends
who cook tastier food
and have that Sunday look about them.

On the bus from Tipon to Cusco
after eating roast guinea pig with the locals
I pretended that I was in church
and that the pungent smell of packed bodies
was incense, an offering
to the one God we all call Father,
that the brown girl staring at my freckled hands
had not yet learned of our sisterhood,
kin, all of us in my holy fantasy,
until I witnessed the exchange.

A man with a boy and a baby
squeezed on board,
standing room only in this rolling temple.
Seamlessly, out of some unseen knowing
the woman to my right raised up her arms.
as the man gently surrendered the baby
into her warmth.
This is my baby
in whom I am well pleased.
take her, hold her
Mother of us all
Pachamama
rock me to sleep
with these people who know things
my people have forgotten.
These people...
...my people.
I want to cry on the crowded bus to Cusco,
House of the Goddess.

When the man was ready to leave
the baby was given back
with one word
"Gracias."
and he went in peace.

Kathleen E. Hanagan, March 6, 2005

Learning to trust

Being away from the States and realizing how much
has been lost in the quest for more, I began to shift. I
dropped into a whole new vibration and learned quickly

that people who are called to Cusco are called for a reason. I began to meet characters with whom I resonated—fellow adventurers, dreamers, renegades, artists, and shamans.

For the first month in Cusco, I lived in an apartment with large glass windows and a breathtaking view of the city and the mountains. What I soon learned is how cold it gets at night when you have thin glass windows and no heat. Though warm during the day, nights could drop below freezing, and the few places that had heat were out of my price range. I brought a down comforter from the States, and purchased an alpaca blanket, hat and gloves with open fingers at the market in Cusco, all of which I needed to stay warm at night. The shower was cold, and the toilet worked sometimes. I was happy in spite of it and accepted these inconveniences of my new life with relative grace. It was, after all, an adventure.

My morning ritual was to jump out of bed and turn on the hot water heater for morning tea, then climb back under the covers to wait. It took a long time for water to boil at 11,000 feet. Once the super-large mug of Irish breakfast tea and milk was in my hands, I relaxed under the covers and stopped shivering so I could eventually drop into meditation. Something different began to happen spontaneously every morning. Rather than my mindfulness meditation, I had conversations with people, both alive and dead. My former lover and I cleared the air about the unkind way we had left each other. My dad apologized for the pain he had caused me as a child, and I let him know that I had forgiven him. My grandmother told me she was proud of me and to remain strong, no matter what happens. I entered into these conversations as if the person were right there in the room. Each time, my heart opened and it seemed as if a weight was lifted from me and the other person. I was doing some serious karmic clearing–or should I say, I was allowing it to happen. High in the Andes, I felt closer to heaven.

A friend who had visited Peru told me of a shaman named Alonso del Rio who lived in Taray, a village near the town of Pisac, an hour away. I set off to find him in the hope of setting up a time to participate in an ayahuasca ceremony.

Ayahuasca, also commonly called yagé, is a brew made out of Banisteriopsis caapi vine, often in combination with other plants. The brew is used as a traditional spiritual medicine in ceremonies among the indigenous people of the Amazon, and is known for its divinatory and healing powers.

I rode the public bus over the mountain to Pisac, the only gringa on board. Amidst the llamas and kiwichi and the full spectrum of life in Peru, I was joyful. I had set myself up to live a wide-open life.

When I arrived in Pisac, I hired a taxi to get to Alonso's place. The extent of my directions were to head toward Taray, turn left onto the narrow bridge, continue straight until I get to a road, walk over the hill, and look for the thatched roof on the right. There will be a German Shepherd dog out front.

Did I say "narrow" bridge? Let me tell you, there is nothing like driving over a hanging bridge in Peru. I have come to love it, and that day, I was breathing deeply for many reasons. I was to meet Alonso, the *ayahuascero,* of whom I had heard good things. Mind you, I was not sure what I was looking for, but I was following the energy of the *loveseed* in my heart.

The taxi driver came to a stop and said that it was the end of the road, pointing to the grassy knoll rising up to an unknown destination. His fingers walked, indicating to me my next mode of transportation. I had only been in Peru for two weeks, so this was new to me—being dropped in the woods with no one around. I had no idea if I was being brave or totally reckless, but I chose to remain utterly hopeful. I decided that I was fully protected. Sure, I was afraid. Yet, I held to the belief that my soul was guiding me and I kept breathing.

Taxi gone. No one around. Water trickling over rocks, green and lush. Quiet. I stopped, my heart pounding. Ahhhhh. I could feel the *loveseed* inside. All is well. Breathe. Look up. Look around. The water is friendly, the rocks are friendly, and the trees are friendly. They are not lost. The air is friendly. You are home here. Onward. Over the hill.

I continued to walk. Over the next rise, the top of the thatched roof appeared. The dog appeared, and children, and a beautiful blond woman and a slightly-built man with the kindest demeanor. This was Alonso's home, with his German-born wife and four handsome children. The man lived in Paradise.

He asked me why I came; why I wanted to drink ayahuasca. I said I have always sought truth and the best way I can serve, and I want guidance that will support me in that quest. We communicated somehow, forming an understanding that he would guide me, that it would be two evenings, and I would stay here with them, fast the day of the ceremony with a day in between where I am free to do whatever I like. I agreed to do that and told him I would be coming with a friend. We shook hands and that was that; date and time set.

Within a few weeks, my friend Heather and I were driving over that narrow bridge, this time to spend several days at Alonso's compound—dogs, children, llamas, and other visitors who would also participate in the ayahuasca ceremonies at night, in the temple. We spent the first day fasting, preparing for the evening to come.

As open as I had felt, nothing much happened for me that first evening. When I met with Alonso the next day, he asked me what I experienced. "No mucho," I said. His response was, "Mas confianza." More trust. He looked at me with deep pool blue eyes. I took him in.

More trust? I had the entire day and the next day fasting to reflect on what it meant to have more trust. I let go of thinking and asked my body. I went for a hike, ate apple strudel at the German restaurant in Pisac, and lay by the river on a blanket for hours, relishing in the experience of being held by Pachamama. I felt nestled in paradise and thought maybe this feeling had to do with more trust. I felt held here by this river, deep in the woods of a little village in Peru. I felt at home. Mas confianza.

When the second ceremony finally arrived, I was as trusting as I knew to be. I felt my own sincerity to know the truth of my own being through this plant. Alonso gave me two drinks that night, and he could see that I was ready. I was.

My main motivation in sharing this with you is to open doors within you that will allow you to know Love personally, as I do. It is in knowing Love as I know her now that inspired me to take a vow. I ask that you suspend needing to understand with your mind, and listen with your heart, as I tell you the rest of the story.

After the second dark drink of jungle roots and herbs, taken in ceremony by candlelight, I settled into my sleeping bag on the dirt floor next to Heather. It was freezing outside and a full moon over the mountain rose nearly straight up just 200 feet away from us. I was cozy in my bag, watching the candlelight dance, as Alonso began to sing the songs about love and the road of stars. I felt held, happy, open, and I declared my total trust. I heard the lullaby.

I quickly moved past the dazzling visions and geometric display. What began as a gentle feeling of joy transformed into an encounter with an energy, a force; what I came to know as a being, feminine in Nature—so strong, benign, protective, breathtakingly beautiful. I simply do not have words to describe her. She called herself Love.

I was taken up by her. The ecstasy I felt as she filled my consciousness was so overwhelming that the last thing I recall saying was, "I had no idea there was this much looooooooove." And then I was gone. I surrendered to her power and we disappeared into one another. I have no idea how long I was with Her. I do not have conscious memory beyond a certain point, until I began to return from wherever I went. At that point, I encountered what appeared to be dark forces. I puffed out my chest, which was filled with Love, and telepathically declared, "You are not real. Only Love is real." I have never felt so grounded and powerful in all my life. I was not afraid. Immediately the dark forces dispersed.

I recall coming back into my body and feeling my arms and hands and smiling like a cat that had just caught a big canary. I was overtaken with joy and began to laugh, and others began to as well. Alonso lit a candle and we all began to dance. It seemed the "journey" part of the night was over, and I had been with Love for four to five hours.

As much as I had felt the power of filial love—love for my parents, my family members, my partner, my children, my friends, my clients, and the world—this direct encounter with Love herself removed all doubt that Love is the power I would consciously live my life by. She was sexy and nurturing, powerful and tender. I would not realize all that such a vow entailed until many years later, when I had to face the parts of me that I had hidden from Her, and yet that were changed forever.

Learning compassion

I encountered many outer challenges, from water dripping onto my computer to rats in the walls and customs that infuriated the logical and goal-driven woman I was. When every attempt to get my wireless service to work failed, over weeks and weeks, I experienced an *amygdala hijack* and flew into a raging temper tantrum right on the sidewalk outside *Telefonica*. I cursed in English and acted out the absolute worst traits of a North American.

It was such a shadow expression of the woman who had come to Peru to penetrate the heart of compassion. I had been so focused on embodying compassion that when I witnessed this happening, I took the *Path of Zero* and surrendered. I showered myself with understanding and empathy, right there on the sidewalk. Arms wrapped around me, rocking back and forth on the ground, on a busy sidewalk in the late morning on a main street in Peru, I told myself that I was really, really brave and that it's really, really hard to live alone in a third world country where you don't even speak the language. I rocked back and forth between the present moment and the pain of my past when I felt totally defeated by my father's rage. Streams of passersby looked on, and I heard the words "loca" and "gringa" more than once. I told myself that I understood that it was not my true intention to be mean and unkind to others who have different ways of doing things, even if they are senseless in my view. I comforted myself as I would comfort a child and began to laugh, and the people began to smile, relieved that the crazy woman with red hair had finally calmed down.

In Peru, seeking to know compassion, I was faced with my total lack of compassion for myself and then others. Even on my sabbatical year, I had fallen into the *Trance* of pushing so hard to get some "work" done and was in complete resistance to what-was. The temper tantrum was my total refusal to accept reality. Byron Katie says in her book *Loving What Is*, "When I argue with reality, I lose—but only 100% of the time." I was losing it!

As I observed my immature and entitled behavior with curiosity and then deep compassion, I pivoted. I simply changed. The loop of awareness was so strong and clear in that moment that I was able to make a huge and lasting shift. Sometimes high drama is what it takes to get our full attention, but ultimately you want to get to the point that the drama is no longer required to get there.

Remember, I had asked to learn about maintaining compassion regardless of circumstance. Here was the answer to my prayer, as I learned experientially what my dear friend Sherry Cupac has told me more than once: "If you are out of compassion for yourself, you are out of compassion for everyone else. If you are out of compassion for others, you are out of compassion for yourself." The world as mirror became very clear to me.

As I began to unwind, I realized how important it was for me to give myself the open space and time of this year, which was the other intention: to feel more spacious inside so that I formed a different relationship with time. I found myself needing to unplug from the shoulds of life, including the "needing to write a book." I read everything about compassion I could get my hands on, and simply allowed myself to learn. I began to relax and instead of writing about the change, I became the change.

Living in the Andes, I learned two important lessons in the Principle of Reciprocity, which is a social rule that says we should repay, in kind, what another person has provided us. In other words, if you give, it will be given back to you. If you have ever given fully of yourself, you know you get more back than you give much of the time. Apply this to your business and life and you will thrive.

The second lesson is harder to master, which is to learn to give without hope of getting anything back. If reciprocity is about getting back what you give, then naturally you may wonder about not having the hope of return. It is when you give without hoping to get anything back that you are giving wholeheartedly. This sets up a very powerful reciprocal response toward you.

Nothing remained the same

After living in Peru for eleven months, I travelled to India for a 30-day meditation retreat at Oneness University. My week travelling alone to holy places in India after the retreat was one of the most sacred times of my life. The entire experience seemed to reorganize my inner world to such a degree that I no longer felt attached to the material world in the same way.

I came home a very different woman, and my life was no longer just about me. I had stepped into a new energy that I later came to identify as the energy of the Solar Feminine. Every aspect of my life began to turn inside out, with new priorities and a growing sense of being called. I was more intentional than ever about my desire to become free of whatever would hold me back from the fullest expression of my *loveseed.*

Enter the Solar Feminine

There is an energy available to all of us that sparks tremendous transformation in every aspect of life, especially those involving sex and relationship, purpose, and money. It changes the shape of marriage, business, religion, politics—really everything.

For women, the relationship to authority is shifting from outside to inside—to our own inner authority. We are beginning to shine our own light and no longer rely on reflected light, as does the moon. This is the potent energy of the Solar Feminine, and as it is being activated in more and more women and men, a beautiful thing is happening on this planet.

We are making the radical shift from the love of power to the power of love. The archetype of Sacred Union is replacing the old myth of separation as we shift from a world based in dualistic thinking to the consciousness of Oneness. Whether you are aware of it or not, you are feeling the effects of this energy, as the Earth receives powerful transmissions of Divine Feminine energy emanating from the Great Central Sun. It is part of the collective field effect of enough people choosing to live in the fifth dimension of consciousness, where there is no fear.

The Solar Feminine is the creative, passionate, focused, pulsating, and radiant feminine energy that is needed on the planet at this time. This is the energized feminine that is fueled by compassion and purpose, and creates powerful positive change, without war. This is the energy I had "downloaded" in Peru.

It is not within the scope of this book to delve into the mysteries surrounding this imbalance of power, but suffice it to say that what we call the gender hierarchy of the patriarchy is only one source of social disparity. Some now prefer to use the word Kyriarchy, a neologism coined by Elisabeth Schussler Fiorenza and derived from the Greek words for "lord" or "master" (kyrios) and "to rule or dominate" (archein). It is best understood as a complex pyramidal system of intersecting social structures of superordination and subordination, of ruling and oppression. The misuse of these fiery solar energies can be seen in the ravages of war, excessive use of fossil fuels, and the degradation of female sexuality.

The lunar qualities of the Feminine—intuition, listening, nurturing, tending—became strong and prevalent during this time, and women have hidden their power in these beautiful gifts of the Divine Feminine for thousands of years. Now we must stop being invisible with those gifts and learn to use our masculine energies to bring them forth into the world. This is the energy that became activated when I was in Peru. It was my Soul setting me on a course that would have me integrate both my shadow and my masculine and feminine energies, becoming who I was always meant to be.

For a woman, fully embodying her Solar Feminine nature has been a huge challenge, requiring great courage. Because women have been conditioned to identify with the Lunar Feminine, when they attempt to express their solar energy, they may model after the Solar masculine, which wreaks havoc with their inner lives and relationships. They push too hard and drive their lives and their health into the ground. I see evidence of the imbalance in my office every day, as driven women with passive men sit on my couch and tell of their misery.

The ensuing battle within every woman has been even more painful than the battle between the sexes. In truth, the first step is putting an end to the war between the nurturing and receptive qualities of her Lunar Feminine energies, and the fierce and fiery qualities of her Solar Feminine. She must first learn to integrate these two.

She must then balance the protective and holding qualities of her Lunar Masculine energies and the driving and ruthless qualities of her Solar Masculine energies. This is the shadow work being asked of all of us today. It is the only real solution to relationship struggles.

Hundreds of thousands of women have been burnt, both literally and figuratively, for stepping out and boldly expressing this powerful energy. The exact figure is not known because records were not kept, but it is estimated that during a 300-year period, between three and five million women were killed and tortured for being witches. How can we not be affected by that?

The complementary energies of the Lunar Masculine are rising at the same time, and men feel the change, too. They have been honing their skills of listening and nurturing, and many are committed to supporting the women in their lives as never before. This very same dance of integration is being asked of men, and often men vacillate between being too passive and then reacting by becoming intimidating or domineering. We must remember that we are all always doing the best we can, and if we knew a better way, we would do better. For that reason, learning a better way is key, and it always has to do with the connection to your own *loveseed*.

Initiation

The energy of the Solar Feminine must be activated in women if we are to bring the planet into balance, but there is often tremendous resistance to do so.

Life often invites us to be activated through some form of *initiation*, which, as I said, can be consciously designed or not. If you have ever felt trapped like a moth in a spider web, then you have been refusing life's invitation to an *initiation*. The trapped condition is there to help you wake up to your power, which is actually in surrender. Maybe you feel trapped by a diagnosis, a bad relationship, an addiction or depression. They are all there to reflect that you are out of alignment with the truth of your power.

Spiritual warriors know that such crises can be both an opportunity for rebirth and the portal through which you can step onto an illumined path that leads to a life of passion, authenticity, and grace. But this requires that you say YES to life and step into the unknown.

Initiation is a shamanic path of transforming emotions such as anger, fear, and despair into love, purity, and compassion. True initiation is always an internal and private act of courage between you and the Divine, whether

191

there is an outer ritual or not. It is the response to Spirit's invitation to discover the greater significance of your life, and at times involves taking a vow.

There are two requirements for archetypal initiation:

1. You must disobey authority or take the road less traveled in order to come to a wisdom and goodness you would not otherwise reach.

2. You must have a strong desire to be the best you can be.

I was definitely on a path of initiation, and the authority I needed to disobey was the driving ambition of my own ego. I was thankfully oblivious to what was ahead, including facing my personal fear factor.

CHAPTER 9

The Fear Factor

"Each of us must confront our own fears, must come face to face with them. How we handle our fears will determine where we go with the rest of our lives. To experience adventure or to be limited by the fear of it."
– Judy Blume

Completing birth

When you make unconscious agreements to adapt to the status quo—which I will call the *upperworld*—you inevitably hide important parts of yourself. If these agreements are left unexamined, the energy you bind up when you hide parts of yourself will eventually create an unbearable tension inside. Whether it is to hide your anger in order to be a good girl or to hide your sensitivity in order to be a tough guy, this tension will cause a kind of dis-ease at some point. You made these agreements or adaptations in order to get whatever nurturance you could in an environment where only parts of you were acceptable. Eventually the good girl gets fed up, or the tough guy has a heart attack. It is so important to take the time to question the agreements that became beliefs that became habits.

More and more over time, what I have found in the clients I work with is that insufficient nurturance and the pace of the digital age have left them feeling as if they are on a treadmill they cannot get off, and that they must keep on keeping on with blinders so as not to be distracted. Rather than take the time to turn inward and make an honest inquiry, they buy into the illusion of not enough time. Rather than take a good look at self, the battle is externalized in crises in four main areas: relationships, health, wealth, and purpose.

Eventually, something stops them in their tracks so they must take a look. In other words, life has a way of presenting you with just the crisis that will take you into the *underworld,* so you can die to your old life and your old self. I call it being reborn in the *underworld*—in that place you have avoided at all costs.

What does it mean to be reborn in the *underworld*? It means you've gone through an experience that has led you to discover parts of you that you had previously never known; shadow parts that carry powerful energy and need to be integrated into the rest of who you are. You have increased your depth by facing an ordeal in which you have chosen life, and thus love, in spite of the suffering, and indeed, as a part of the suffering. As a result, you've developed a heart of wisdom, courage, and love. You now take everything in the *upperworld* with a grain of salt—not with indifference, but with less attachment to outcome and greater respect for the mystery of existence.

Birth itself is a kind of *underworld* wrought with primitive and basic instincts. You go back to that, to the truth of your life, to complete your birth. As one of my most important spiritual teachers, Steven Levine, said in an interview. "... becoming fully born... most people live with one foot in the womb, hopping around the world, never quite coming out. Completing our birth is a process of becoming grounded, putting both feet on the ground. It is taking responsibility for being born, but not responsibility as blame.... We are not responsible for our incarnation, we are responsible to our incarnation."

Drop the banana

In India, my biggest prayer was to own whatever would keep me from taking full responsibility for my life. While on a 30-day silent retreat, I discovered that my mind was like a wild monkey, and I incessantly judged everyone and everything, beginning with myself. I had never witnessed it quite in the same way, as the longest silent retreat I had been on previously was 10 days. But now I got to watch the carnival! You could say it was the dark shadow of the compassionate therapist I had identified with, and it was quite shocking. I practiced letting go of each judgment as it arose, except at lunch, where just eating a mouthful of the daily gruel required a large measure of surrender.

While walking back to my dorm room from lunch one day, I saw a fellow participant in the distance—a woman with a banana. A wild monkey leapt off the building, where the sly characters hung out to taunt humans, and attempted to grab the banana. I could hardly believe my eyes when I saw the woman grabbing her banana back, which really pissed off the monkey, as evidenced by the increasing intensity of screeching sounds coming from the creature. As I approached her I screamed, "Drop the banana. Let it go. Don't fight the monkey!" I could see exactly what *she* needed to do and would soon have plenty of opportunity myself to practice not fighting the monkey.

When I arrived home after being away a year, I faced a monumental challenge: I needed to resuscitate my practice and begin making money. I needed to put both feet back on the ground.

I adopted a way of dealing with challenge that I would never have been able to prior to my journey. The transition was hard on every level, but as I devoted myself to the task, more and more clarity appeared. I found a home of my own and as the weather warmed, I began the task of clearing the land and making sense of the landscaping, which was under two years of oak leaves from the massive trees towering over the property. I became a gardener and a builder of paths and ponds and walls and magical sitting areas. I realize now that this was a way to remain connected to the earth and helped ground me through a crisis of faith I did not see coming.

Beyond faith

I would say that I have always been a woman of faith—deep faith—in Spirit. I can never recall reaching a point of not believing in some force greater than myself, but I was about to go there. Apparently, I needed to know that part of me too—the part that finds no meaning in anything. I am sure that many of you have met that part—the part that frankly doesn't care if there is a God or not.

As my new home took shape into a place of beauty, I began to wonder why I had even bought it. I kept fantasizing about living in a dirt hut in the Himalayas and returning to the very simple life I had grown to love during my year away. All the consumption was weighing me down, and I judged the entire project of home and garden renovations far too extravagant for who I had become.

In late May, a suffocating darkness came over me. It was as if my soul was crying, longing for a place to rest. My best friend called one day, knowing I was struggling. Her genuine attempts to support me were met with my nihilism. Financial burden coupled with exhaustion from all the work had brought me to my knees, but I could no longer pray to the God I once knew. I questioned every thought and every concept, and a great doubt rose up in my soul.

I was so angry that this was happening, after a life in which I had consciously cultivated faith. The shadow of my bright faith was a bottomless well of darkness that initially felt like an empty deadness. Soon came the fury of my resistance and the suffering that accompanies it, until I remembered to drop the banana.

No one and nothing was of any comfort, except gardening. The garden became my ashram, where I felt an intimate connection with the earth. So that is where I lived, in between clients, working from morning until late at night, often under spotlights so I could see. When the dark thoughts and feelings arose, I faced them, then let them go, digging and planting and arranging, my hands in the dirt as often as possible. I bludgeoned roots with a shovel, releasing the rage that was rising up within me and making room for new plantings. The earth nourished me in some silent way.

The Temple

There are gifts to be mined in every depression, every descent into the place where your soul refuses to conform. Not only did I shake loose any concepts from the "God of our father's" faith, which may have been lingering, but I also learned a new language. I discovered that the earth speaks to us in a language beyond words, and I could feel her in a way similar to the way I felt her when I was a child and spent endless hours alone in the woods. I call these messages *uploads*, because that is exactly what was happening, on a cellular level.

She (the earth) told me that my new home was not just for me, so I could relax about it being so extravagant. She said it was for the community; a place to gather people to bring in the new energies. Everything was beginning to make sense now, and I understood why I had bought the house in the first place. Again I said YES.

Before long, I found myself in training as a priestess and taking an official vow to usher in the New Earth. My psychotherapy practice thrived again, and I invited healers from other areas of the country to stay with me and offer their services to my community.

The Temple was magnificent, and I delighted in its upkeep. To live in a place with so much light, both literally and figuratively, was a joy. I felt on-purpose, was healthier than ever due to all the gardening, and my finances had stabilized. The creativity and celebration of this time invited many new connections, and I could feel myself growing like a plant that is sufficiently nourished.

Another call

It happened anyhow, receiving that call—the call that disrupts the homeostasis of the moment. In 2000, I had a reading by a wise Mayan woman who told me that my work was to reach many people. I didn't understand at the time, as the internet was new and I had no context for working virtually. I began to explore possibilities and took a class with a business coach who tried to help me articulate the benefit people received from my work. I was frustrated beyond belief, but the truth is, I was afraid that I did not have that much to offer. There was a rattling inside that I could not explain.

I have always given myself the gift of going on retreat, which has served me well—helping to disarm the uber-responsible side of my personality so I could descend into unexplored territory. I decided to take a trip to the jungle of Brazil, where I would be involved in sacred rituals and Butoh Dance. Butoh, a form of Japanese dance theatre, is known to "resist fixity" and is difficult to define. Some features of the art form include taboo topics, playful and grotesque imagery, extreme or absurd environments—very shadow-like in its essence. Take note that travelling to less civilized parts of the planet where senses are stimulated in new ways and you maintain a stronger connection to the earth invites callings and shadow work. Adventures disrupt the *Trance*, and you begin to remember things you had forgotten.

Each person in the retreat did their own Butoh dance at week's end. My dance, unbeknownst to my conscious mind, was a foretelling of the journey ahead as I stripped down to nothing but underwear, smeared my body with white powder and streaks of green, and climbed into a tall tree.

The thing with a Butoh dance is that you don't really know ahead of time what on God's green earth you are going to do. There may be a vague sense, but if you are fully present to the dance, something rises up from the depths of your unconscious, and you enter into entirely new territory.

I began grunting, wildly shaking the branches, and a strange sensation of terror came over me. I haven't much mentioned being afraid because the truth is, throughout my life I rarely felt fear. Other than worrying about not having enough money, which I compensated for by working hard to assure myself that I had enough, I always managed to put fear back into the bag.

I had been counter-phobic since the age of four, when my father scared me terribly by threatening to hang me outside a second-floor window. I had called my mother because I could not sleep, and she came upstairs to comfort me. I recall my legs being so restless, still unable to sleep. When I called her again, my father stormed up the stairs and picked me up by my pajamas. I remember the jolt, facing the floor, his one arm tightly holding me at my ribs. "If you call your mother one more time, I'll drop you out this goddamned window." I closed my eyes and all I really remember was hearing the rumble of my father's elbow attempting to lift the screen of the hallway window and the deafening sound of terror in my head.

At age four, I did not know that my father would never do that and loved me deeply, however much I pushed his buttons more than any of my siblings. As my lips quivered beyond control, I sucked in my breath, bit my bottom lip, and swallowed the fear. The quivering stopped, and all I could feel was rage and deep shame. The fear went deep into my shadow, beneath the rage and the shame, until that day in the tree.

American poetess Mary Oliver writes in "The Uses of Sorrow" from *Thirst*, "Someone I loved once gave me a box full of darkness. It took me years to understand that this too, was a gift." This gift I received from my father of living a "fearless" life had blessed me with a spirit of curiosity and adventure, unlike most people I knew. It was now time to get to the bottom of the gift, where fear had been hiding all this time. On some level I knew this and surrendered to the dance.

I didn't want to leave the tree and whatever it symbolized. I clung to the trunk, making noises that didn't sound human. When we are wounded so young, we often don't have recognizable language for how we feel. I sensed the downward pull, and as I howled sounds of protest, the group below began to chant and the drummers drummed faster and louder. I began my descent, viscerally feeling a wild terror inside me. Down I climbed, the music deafening.

As I made contact with the ground, I looked up and saw another tree, much lower to the ground, with a huge, hanging bunch of cascading berries. I knew that tree was my destination and began to focus in its direction. I was one with the music, the group, the ground, and the entire experience. Leaving the pointy plants, I crawled up to the tree as the group began to sing a new song. The drums slowed down, and I effortlessly lifted my body, placing my head into the crown of hanging berries, facing outward toward the group. Nature cooperates so beautifully when we surrender control.

My heart was pounding, and I felt totally exposed as I sat mostly naked as the Queen of the Jungle. I leapt into the arms of the oldest woman there, Harriett, who cradled and covered me. I peeked back at all of them and saw only love.

Upon returning to the Temple after the retreat, everything felt different. As in the Bee Gees song *Massachusetts*, I felt the urge to go home.

Forty years prior, in spite of my father's disapproval, I left Massachusetts with my hair on fire to explore the world outside. After the retreat in Brazil, I simply knew I needed to return while Mom and Dad were still alive. I didn't even question it, and I had a loose plan as to how I would keep myself going.

No more water in the pot

I put the Temple on the market, but before leaving, I had one final gathering—a residential weekend of sexual healing with 14 women. My friend Vyana and I combined our priestess talents, offering a deep-dive to help these women reclaim and integrate their repressed and diluted sexuality. It was edgy, intense, and ever-so-powerful and beautiful.

I had never lived like a woman with Puritan roots, which may explain some of my feelings of not quite belonging in Massachusetts. After the workshop, I was tired, but deeply satisfied with not only the workshop, but also my decision to let the Temple go. Again, many people questioned me and asked why in the world I would put so much into a place and then leave. By that point in my life, I recognized when my soul was speaking, and simply said so. My soul wanted me to move on.

The tiredness I felt soon turned to exhaustion, but I had to pack, and there was my psychotherapy practice to close once again. By week's end, I was in the hospital, flat on my back with an IV, about to go into intensive care. I had a kidney infection and was becoming septic.

When I visited my acupuncturist Eli in Gloucester, he said my condition was as if there is a pot on a hot stove with no water in it—eventually the pot burns. Obviously, I was way out of balance.

Saving myself

All the pushing and excessive use of pushing energy in my lifetime, coupled with the huge task of leaving the Temple, both physically and emotionally, provided the perfect storm of conditions that I became depleted and nearly collapsed. After two days in the hospital, the night nurse came in and said, "Honey, we'll be taking you to ICU soon. You aren't getting any better, and we're afraid you'll become septic." I had barely enough energy to comprehend what she was saying, but I did. In that very moment, I reached into an invisible reservoir, connected to my heart, and decided to pivot. It was a decision I recall making in the form of a prayer, and it wasn't a prayer of supplication but rather of defiance. It went like this: *NO. NO. NO WAY will I go into ICU. Get me out of here. Help me. Help. Help. Help.* Everything in me was reaching for the invisible help I needed at the moment.

I was scared and strong at the same time. I was angry to be there, and the energy of my anger helped me. Anger has more power than fear, as you will recall from the Map of Consciousness. Anger was not in my shadow, but rather like a dear friend I had come to terms with over the years. But the fear was in my shadow, and I could not let it win. There is a time for surrender and a time for battle, so I called on the troops.

I managed to avoid ICU, and after five days, went back to the Temple with a severely distended belly that felt as hard as marble. I showed the nurse before being discharged and she seemed indifferent but I sensed something was wrong. Lying in bed that night, I felt as if I would explode with a pressure and pain accompanied by the feeling of intense fear. I had experienced enough shamanic healing to know that I could ask for another kind of help.

Instinctively, I began to pull the stagnant energy out of my belly. At first there was nothing, but then I felt a black snake-like energy that I grabbed with both hands and began pulling out, fist over fist. It was thick, black and it kept coming and coming. I realized that this was mine, and it also belonged to the women from the sexual healing workshop, and it belonged to all of humanity. It was the heavy black stagnant energy of fear we have ingested, and I felt better and better as I pulled it out. My belly softened and became a normal size, and I finally fell asleep feeling like my own hero. I was 58 and about to begin a new life, again.

Massachusetts

The highlights of my time in Massachusetts were the moments sitting at the kitchen table with my mother and father, listening to the stories of their lives after one of Mom's home-cooked meals. I was now alone with them, something I had not experienced since my sister was born in 1954. I sat with them for at least one meal a day for almost a year before moving into my own apartment. Those sweet moments are etched like delicate scrimshaw on my heart.

Want and hope. I could feel both in all their stories. In my generation for sure, and lingering into the next, is this profound fear of—and illusion of—shortage, scarcity, not-enoughness.

The ability to adapt and conform in order to survive is always at play. Many people do it well, seem to live lives free from shortage and enjoy life to the hilt. I worked long, hard hours with countless clients so that I had little time to even feel the scarcity. I recreated my childhood of being the oldest—the one watching out for everyone. I continuously felt the "too muchness" of my life until I could not keep up with the illusion that I had it all together. If this is what "success" felt like, I was not sure I wanted to keep up the good work my generation had learned.

I was exhausted by the time I arrived in Massachusetts, and all I wanted to do was rest. I had paid a huge amount of money to an online marketing coach, a woman 25 years younger than I who functioned like the "Energizer bunny" and who told me to go to early morning business networking meetings to promote myself. She had mastered this formula for success: a system for attracting clients that promised to grow a list of admirers who eventually would become paying clients. She touted what sounded like good sense based on the Universal Law of Attraction, and by all appearances she was a spiritually-wise woman.

Ah, the trap of appearances—another illusion that comes when we project authority outward. As conflicted as I was, I fell into the trap of giving up my power to someone who did not see me and thus could not really guide me. I recall the first brief coaching phone call where I confessed that I felt terrified. She asked me why, and I said that I did not know. I did not. I could only feel it, and she didn't have a clue how to help me, so she did what most people do when faced with someone's fear—she told me there was nothing to be afraid of, and that I just needed to "get out there." I was still in total denial that I had spent years becoming an expert at something I loved very much. I had not even grieved the loss of my business, and I imagined I could walk away from all of it without reckoning with fear. Such is the nature of an emotional blind spot.

In the course of the past several years, the story I tell of this time is of a wise woman who lived in a hut in the woods with herbs and poultices for the spirit. She didn't announce what she did, because she had been doing it for so long that the people knew who she was. They came from far and wide to sit with her, because her presence was healing in and of itself. She was forced, for some unknown reason that only her soul knew, to leave her hut and all her tools of the trade behind and wander for many years, bereft, until she realized the only tool she needed was inside her.

Surviving the witch hunt this time

I found it impossible to keep up the pace needed to succeed in the program. My heart raced when I tried to sleep, and I would lie awake night after night, listening to the tide. I thought if I pushed harder, bought one more helpful program, or went to one more conference to learn one more method for success, I would finally be enough.

With not enough yin and too much yang, my health declined. There I was in mad pursuit of a big list of people to dazzle and to eventually charge huge amounts of money for my expertise, when in truth, I felt as if I had nothing to offer by that point. I knew that this was not why I left the Temple, and a powerful veil of amnesia spread over me. I had forgotten who I really was.

I saw so many women and some men in the programs who were not accustomed to the hard sell, particularly the "healers." Many got sick in the process, or just plain angry. We were taught to market to people's pain, and I began to feel less and less alive as I attempted to do what I was being taught, as my own pain was becoming unbearable.

After a year, I moved to Salem and lived on the wharf, near the site of the Salem witch trials. It was a bleak time in every way, and no matter where I turned in the online marketing world, it seemed that the values I held dear were not to be found. I felt lost, without a compass, and my heart was breaking. I witnessed the feminine values of connection and empathy being talked about, but in truth, I experienced mountains of caterpillars stepping on one another to get to the top.

Yet, I was too afraid to stop. I had invested so much time and money already, and besides, I had left my tools behind. I went into a painful trance that depleted my confidence, and I eventually sought another teacher. Coming from desperation, I chose teachers who would mirror my inadequacies.

One of the exercises I had to complete was to ask former clients what they valued about working with me. Each time, the word "soul" came up. I felt hopeful about this, and I told one of the coaches I had hired when she asked me what my expertise was. I said that, essentially, I am a spiritual teacher and help people connect with their souls. Her response was, "Who do you think you are, Eckhart Tolle?" I was crushed.

There were many moments I wanted to die. I felt like a fraud and a total failure. I attempted to connect with my former high school friends who still lived in the area, but I found nothing in common with them. Many were just retiring after being teachers for 40 years, and on several occasions, eyes glazed over if I shared what I was up to. In fact, one formerly-close friend hurled a gut-wrenching accusation at me that I was "selling spirituality." I was already so raw, and it cut like a knife.

We have a hard time really believing in ourselves as long as we've not faced our fear. The full potential of our *loveseed* cannot be released until we do. This requires surrender—the *Path of Zero*—allowing ourselves to get to nothing, whatever that means for us individually. Anything short of this does not allow us to open to the bigness of who we are, as we continue to dress up our feelings of inadequacy.

It's different for everyone. Fear is deeply personal and at the same time entirely universal. All fear is truly a fear of the Self. Once you face it, you are in the home stretch of your life, where you can look into the distance and be sure that the best version of you will show up, no matter how old you are. This allows the future to be bright, no matter what you are enduring in this moment. I began to understand this more and more.

After a year in Salem, I took a pause from the new coach I had been working with whose laser focus was on making money. She mocked the more spiritual members of the program, and once I began to witness her cruelty toward several people, I stepped way back and questioned my involvement. I had to face the greed in my shadow as I realized I would not have been drawn to this woman if I did not resonate with her on some level. I was both drawn to and repelled by her, which is a sign that I was in shadow territory. Sure, I wanted to do good things for others with the money, but I temporarily abandoned my core values out of my disempowered idea that she knew the way. It hurt to face this truth.

Heavy-hearted, I went on retreat in North Carolina, staying with my friend Lavon in the Smoky Mountains for several months. I gathered myself and began to feel hopeful again. My creativity and focus returned, and I was guided to work with a director to write and perform a one-woman show. Irony of ironies, one of the characters was an outrageous bag lady who was willing to die for love. As I engaged in this pursuit, my savings dwindled, and more fear began to set in.

Out of desperation, I sought the help of a remarkable woman who did see my light and with whom I did the work of deeply reconnecting to my soul. I set forth my firm intention to do my part to help as many people as possible to turn on their light. That was my new brand—*turn on your light*—which I claimed at the very moment my own light was greatly dimming. I was too afraid to turn back at that point.

I know now that it was a rebirth and not a rebranding that I needed, but this claiming of my soul's purpose helped anchor the vision that I have held since. It was instrumental in giving me the courage to refuse to abandon my calling.

The belly of the beast

In North Carolina I got my hands in the dirt again and built some gardens, which brought me back to center. At the thought of returning to Massachusetts from North Carolina, I lost all my energy, which was a good sign that I needed to course correct. I decided to move to Portland, Oregon, where my oldest daughter lived. The plan was to return to my former work and build a new practice.

Twenty-five years earlier, in Northern Virginia, I had built my thriving psychotherapy practice without a website and virtually no marketing, other than word of mouth and giving a few free workshops. Portland was an entirely different reality, where managed care rules the day in mental health, and where people, for the most part, either go hiking, drink beer, or get Tarot readings to feel better. That latter statement is an exaggeration, but true nonetheless. I soon discovered that doing business on the West Coast is far different from doing business in the affluent bubble of Northern Virginia.

Every professional door I knocked on in Portland either didn't open or blew back in my face. I was now 61 years old and walking the razor's edge as never before, hoping not to fall into the belly of the beast—that part of the *Heroine's Journey* where the hero fights the dragon or is plunged deep into enemy territory. It's also when she confronts her worst fears.

I moved to Portland, in part, to be near my oldest child, Antje, whom I deeply loved. Within weeks of being there, she stopped communicating with me but would not tell me why. Clearly, external circumstances were propelling me toward a slippery slope, as the gravitational force of downward pull began to take hold.

No matter what I did to mend the relationship with my daughter, she remained angry at me. My heart was breaking over this chasm between us. To avoid bankruptcy, I moved in with friends and began to look for a job for the first time in 25 years. I had always taken pride in working for myself, but now I would shed that identity, too. That was hard enough, but I did not see ageism coming as I still considered myself vital. No matter where I applied, no one was interested.

After months, I finally found a rookie job in a medical clinic sitting in a room with no windows that was so cold by the time lunch came that my fingers were blue. I saw eight to nine people per day who had never seen a psychotherapist and whose lives were packed with pain and the effects of abuse. I earned less in a day than I had earned in one hour in my former life, but the miracle (shift in perception) was happening. I was once again doing what I loved, and my spirit became stronger.

My father was dying during this time, and the grief over that loss added to my capacity to surrender. During one of the many visits to see Dad, I went for a treatment by Eli, my trusted acupuncturist, to help with my inflamed knees. I was so afraid that this bilateral condition was the beginning of rheumatoid arthritis, the same disease from which my paternal grandmother was crippled most of her life.

He was concerned, and I felt the compassion of this true healer. When I asked him if he thought it was rheumatoid arthritis, he gently placed his hand on my legs and said, "You still have a choice." Eli was right about that.

I heard voices during this time—voices that said I was a loser at 61-years-old, in declining health, living with friends in a subsistence-level job, and on Obamacare. I heard them say much worse than that, and I questioned everything the voices said. I had a choice as to whether I wanted to buy into the narrative that made me into a "has been" with nothing more to offer the world. These were the voices I had spent all my money paying people to save me from.

I experienced myself as totally invisible and insignificant at some moments, yet there was this overarching knowing that I was experiencing exactly what I needed to. I trusted this in the deepest part of my being, in my *loveseed,* and I nurtured that connection in every way I could.

As I shed my old identity, I reached the point where I had lost the last vestige of cultural approval for who I thought I was. I was now broke, broken, and living with friends. Only Self-as-Heart can go beyond this kind of failure, which prepared me to write this book. Getting to *Zero* was my liberation through a knowing of my heart.

CHAPTER 10

A Knowing of the Heart

"I am not bound to win, but I am bound to be true.
I am not bound to succeed, but I am bound to
live up to what light I have."
— Abraham Lincoln

The inner presence

One of the benefits of losing all material worth is that you are visited by a blessed guest who questions everything, which results in a galvanizing clarity about what is really important. It's as if the Wise Sage moves in and begins to make choices. You come to know in your bones that your Soul has your back.

Losing everything can be a point of power in a person's life. In the ashes of what was, you begin to discern what could never be destroyed. If you can put your arms around yourself in the midst of loss, you enter a portal of grace to another world where you notice every kindness and every gift. You begin to make friends with your own life. A new humility takes shape, and you become deeply grateful.

Love and wisdom are our primary obligations in life, and everything that happens gives us the opportunity to act from love and learn from experience. When we act from our true desire, we will always choose love, for that is who we are. When you find your circumstances mirroring back scarcity and ill health, as I had, the sooner you can shift your attention from circumstances to your true self, your *loveseed*, the better. Your *loveseed* is the Inner Presence—the Source of Infinite Prosperity.

Discernment

We must learn to discern our true desire from the pressure that comes from within and face our fears and limiting beliefs that are meant to maintain conformity. It is as *simple* as that, and I say that tongue in cheek, because in practice it turns out not to be so simple.

You begin by realizing that circumstances are mirroring back to you what is true for you, and if what you have is not what you want, then you need to get clear about your desire. You may have bought into someone else's dream for you, or even bought into someone else's dream for themselves, because you were not clear about yours.

The practice of discernment is an aspect of higher consciousness, and not just a step up from judgment, but its opposite. Through judgment you reveal what you still need to confront and learn. Through discernment, you reveal what you have mastered. This is wisdom, and I was on a crash-course.

A young child at the age of four tries on countless roles, from mom and dad to Superman, Wonder Woman, and every sort of magical character. This is natural at this developmental stage and a time when the need for mirroring is very basic.

In shedding an identity as I did in leaving the Temple, I had put myself in the situation of seeking a new identity. It was in fact, a common game played in coaching circles to have the entire group of 120 people line up to take a turn at the microphone declaring what kind of superhero or superheroine they were.

Whenever this happened, I felt uneasy, not because it wasn't interesting, but because I didn't know. I also sensed that the knowing would come from inside me and not in an attempt to give the hotshot elevator speech declaring the benefits potential clients would receive from me—and according to these teachings, everyone was a potential client. There was an ulterior motive to every encounter. This was not my way, and the message was *If you want to make money, get out of your own way and do what I say.* In other words, surrender to me—a kind of Guru of the Dollar to be emulated. I began to doubt myself, just as I did 57 years earlier when someone who loved me scared me to my core, and I watched it happen while feeling helpless to do anything about it.

Like a good four-year-old, I kept asking questions and checking in with my own *loveseed.* What I experienced in the rah-rah of the online marketing world felt very uncomfortable, and we were told that we needed to step out of our comfort zones and take "massive action," a kind of uber-masculine approach to life. I did not trust the knowing of what did not feel right and began to doubt my every thought. I felt totally lost. I had taken on too many moves, too many changes, and found myself looping back on a real heroine's journey to an earlier time when my own natural process of forming an identity was interrupted by trauma.

This trauma happens for all of us in some way, and then our suffering unfolds as a result of mistaken identity, often one failure after the other. We forget that we are co-creators with the Divine, the Source of all—multidimensional beings with a sacred mission—and that we have everything we need inside. At the same time we need one another to fulfill our purpose on Earth.

Not to worry, though. If you never make any mis-takes, you are not taking enough risks, which would lead you to view failure in an entirely different light. Napoleon Hill, author of the classic *Think and Grow Rich* wrote, "Every adversity, every failure and every heartache carries with it the seed of an equivalent or a greater benefit."

There is a power to accepting defeat consciously, however, that has nothing to do with failure. People in 12-Step Programs know this on a gut level, as their true success arises from that acceptance of defeat, which is surrender. This frees up oceans of energy that are bound up in battle to then be used in the service of the next step we are asked to take.

Wisdom comes from learning the lessons that mis-takes have afforded and forgiving yourself for getting off course. In therapeutic circles, that is called an AFGA– another fucking growth opportunity–which you can only have once you cease blaming anyone or anything. This ownership is a source of liberation that leads to wisdom. We can take comfort in what Pema Chodron says about failure from her audio recording entitled *Fail, Fail Again, Fail Better*, "Failure opens an unguarded, vulnerable and wide-open space. And from that space the best part of ourselves comes out."

Remember the design

We must remember the design, the bigger context, so we can be held in place as we experience the full range of life, from ecstatic joy to deep despair. Many of you live like that, even recklessly. Others wish you had more of it. We are all trying to find our balance.

I have a tattoo on my left wrist that says "Remember the Design." It was a big commitment to get it. I believe that my commitment to wake up has had to be fierce, given what I now know about the terror I have been running from as long as I can remember. I also had to make friends with the real and learn the value of limits. In essence, we must all dethrone our narcissism to come home to the *true self.*

Limits keep us safe while we are learning to love ourselves, but some of us tend toward recklessness, which is really anger turned toward the self. Without fully forgiving ourselves for our mis-takes, we may continue to repeat them and fail to be protective of ourselves and actually learn from fear. Fear gets a bad rap, but it can be the beginning of wisdom.

I have come to feel a cringe when a friend says, "You defy gravity" to compliment me, because I don't want to put energy into defying anything, least of all gravity. I accept gravity. I have learned limits, yet I will continue to dance at the edges. That is the way some of us are made, as we peer into the future and bring back what we learn.

Making friends with the real also means that you learn to discern between the story in your mind and what is really happening. You re-associate feelings that you dissociated long ago, and you come into present time. You learn that life is simply happening; not to you—it simply is happening. And you claim your right as a co-creator when you choose how to respond. You reclaim your sense of being a creator when you become fully intentional, shedding the beloved victim stance that almost every person carries at some point. This entails the work of reconnection to the *loveseed*, which always involves the shedding of what is not real.

After all those years of helping others do that, I was back to the drawing board in relation to myself, and I renewed my intention to allow love to lead my life. The reason this is so important—and why many spiritual teachers tell you over and over to renew your intention to let love lead—is that it is so easy to get distracted and diverted from your most holy and important of obligations.

An obligation can be seen as a legal duty, or as a "debt of gratitude for a service or favor." I mean it in the latter sense, as the gratitude you give back to life. When you do this—when you commit to bring your attention back to Love, your true nature, the expression of that Love flows through you continuously and abundantly, in the way your soul intended when you chose to come to Earth—you won't run out of anything.

Gravity and grace

There is a wonderful Greek word, *enantiodromia*, which is a moment of radical shift where you look at denied parts of yourself to come back into balance. I love to speak it aloud dramatically, because the meaning and the energy of the word itself are in synch. It is a principle that says the superabundance of any force inevitably produces its opposite—similar to the principle of equilibrium in the natural world—where restoration of balance is the driving principle.

But Jung took it further to say that a thing psychically transmogrifies—which means to transform in a surprising or magical manner—into its shadow opposite when there has been a repression of psychic energy. That energy is then experienced as something outside of one's self that is powerful and threatening to the person. In my case, the outer world was pointing me back to own and embrace my terror of not-enoughness on every level—not enough money, energy, power, love, time, and worth.

Certainly, not everyone needs to lose everything to face their fear, but my soul was intent upon getting my attention this time. **The difference between the downward pull and the Path of Zero is that the downward pull is all that is not you pulling you to become other than who you truly are,**

while the Path of Zero means surrendering all that is not you to become who you truly are.

Living on planet Earth has always been a balancing act of gravity and grace. As the mystic and political activist Simone Weil says in *Gravity and Grace*, "All the natural movements of the soul are controlled by laws analogous to those of physical gravity. Grace is the only exception. We must always expect things to happen in conformity with the laws of gravity unless there is supernatural intervention." This movement of grace is the movement of Love radiating in all possible directions into the field of infinite possibility (eros). Each of us comes from that field, the one "beyond wrongdoing and rightdoing," as Rumi says.

The Spiritual Law of Grace speaks of Grace as a kind of Divine expression of mercy bestowed upon human beings. It dissolves karma, changes matter, and creates miracles. Our Divine selves, or Souls, accepted the awesome opportunity to become embodied beings on the Earth-plane to experience life as fully as possible, particularly the emotions we feel. We are always at choice, having free will to co-create our lives to the most beautiful and perfect expression of our desires.

When we invoke the Spiritual Law of Grace—to transmute and uplift our emotional feelings to heal our relationships, bodies, and even our financial struggles through prayer— we must open ourselves to receive. Your prayer causes you to focus, and the Law of Attraction causes everything in the Universe that's in vibrational harmony with your focus to come to you. Yet, as the American novelist, Flannery

O'Connor says, "All human nature vigorously resists grace because grace changes us and change is painful."

We have created whatever situations we are in with our very own consciousness, and as we learn the lesson from each experience, we can then open ourselves to Grace and receive it.

We can, in fact, offer Grace to others through compassion, empathy, forgiveness, mercy, and love. Each time we do this we open our hearts to receive an inflow of Divine love and mercy, which is truly supernatural intervention.

From the very beginning, you may not have had the support to thrive in that field and be the recipient of "supernatural intervention." As a result, the forces of the downward pull exerted tremendous control over your life. That Is why I am writing this book. I know how it feels to see your entire life unravel before your eyes and to feel helpless to do anything about it. Just as I discovered for myself, I know that the vibration of the field is still inside you, nestled in your *loveseed.* Even without ever meeting you, I know that to be true, and that deeply connects us.

The unconscious mind takes orders, but it doesn't make decisions. That is up to us, to that ineffable and infinite power that is our true nature. My unconscious mind had apparently believed a whole lot of messages about being insignificant and had taken orders to create a life that reflected that. I felt trapped, helpless and hopeless—like a 4-year-old being hung out a window. At the same time, I knew I was beginning to heal, as I could finally witness and have compassion at the depth of my own fear.

Humiliation or humility

The mind is found in every cell of the body, and when we are chronically negative or in conflict with ourselves, the body reacts. It has a kind of super-wisdom within, and often breakdowns in the immune system occur as the body reacts to that which is not the truth of the person. The occasional negative thought does not hurt the body, because the body is inclined toward health, but the chronic thought, whether conscious or unconscious, has an affect.

I became less and less able to tolerate the dysfunction in the system I was working in and the poverty I was experiencing. Yes, I did have to contend with the voice of my Inner Critic that said things like *You are a total loser. Look at you, without a pot to pee in. What a mess you are. Over the hill. A total failure.* This attachment to feeling humiliated comes from being over-identified with some ideal version of ourselves—our ego. I did my best not to indulge in self-pity, but I would not be human if at times I had not. I prayed to be humble enough to learn what I needed to learn.

My mother became incredibly important to me during this time. I have always loved and respected my mother, but I had shared her with six younger siblings and my demanding father. I learned to be as self-reliant as I could be. I knew she had her hands full, and part of my adaptation was to be as helpful as possible and need as little as possible.

But this time I needed her support. I felt so ashamed at times—so weak both physically and emotionally, so broke and broken, that I really did not feel I could turn to anyone else. If she had not helped me out in many ways, I could easily have ended up as a bag lady, a psychic fear of mine of archetypal proportions. So many good people do, and I was acutely aware of the blessings of having a mother like mine during this time.

She listened and continued to remind me that I had a bigger purpose and that my pain was for a reason. Consider the irony of my mother being the one there for me at this most difficult time in my life, which was during the year after my father died. My own psychic death was happening during the time my father was dying, and his dying helped to teach me even more about the power of surrender. All that I was going through alongside my father dying brought me to my knees, and my world began to tip. It opened up space for my mother to be there for me in a new way. Who could possibly have orchestrated such a healing?

My mother's voice nourished the voice of my *Compassionate Witness*, which goes something like this: *You have always deserved better than this. It is a fine mess you've gotten yourself into, but you will write about it some day and help a few other people who feel as if they have come to the end of the road. Good work. You made some awesome mis-takes, and you have been willing to do whatever it takes to learn. You never knew you were this afraid, but you were, and you acted bravely in spite of the fear. Now you've learned how to love that part of you, and you really don't need to stay stuck here any longer.*

This is a kind of loving, healthy pride that is unlike the entitlement of narcissism and lets you know your innate worthiness. You are not worse or better than anyone else, and you can call on it even when you are otherwise feeling hopeless. On Hawkins's scale of emotions, it is the energy right before courage when you begin to make change. Healthy pride is the fuel you need to pivot toward your true desire. It is the deservedness we were born with, all of us, and we didn't need to do a thing to earn it.

On one of the days I was feeling healthy pride, I got myself fired for speaking truth to power. The circumstances around my getting fired—for the first time in my life—are so utterly bizarre that when it happened I immediately realized I was being nudged to move on and felt a huge relief. It was a soul move, for sure.

Just as quickly, I realized that I had not been paid, and that would be a problem. Fear set in. I remember it so vividly. I was trembling and trying to figure out a plan in my head—trying to gain control. I realized what I was doing and remembered I cannot find any answers in my head, so I turned in to my feelings—and I was really angry.

I railed against God and all the powers that be and screamed that I had done everything I was nudged, guided, and prompted to do. I had answered the call, faced fear after fear, and had gotten more broke and more broken in the process—all for what? *What good has it all been? What the hell did you want me to learn, to achieve or to master? I have made one damn mistake after the other and picked myself up each time. Damn, give me a break. Tell me what to do next, because I have no fucking idea. I need your help. I am not doing anything until I hear from you!*

Huh! There it was. The shadow of my self-reliance. I let go of the reins, got into my car to go to an appointment, and after 20 minutes I heard a voice—yes, I heard a very clear voice—say, "Go back to northern Virginia."

I took a breath, said, "Thanks. Let me try that out," and then checked in, breathing into my heart. I got a big YES. I was so grateful. I would return to where I began, having lost everything and gained so much. This was *enantiodromia!* A year before I would have felt humiliated to do so, but now I felt humble enough to return, knowing that my connection to what was important had never been severed. Humiliation is about you, while humility is about surrendering to something far greater than yourself.

I called my sister Peggy right away, and true to her optimistic and supportive nature, she said, "Great. I knew you were coming back. You can stay with us."

I felt wholehearted at last. I would return "home."

Full-spectrum living

I finally embraced full-spectrum living, which required that I face my fear, anger, sadness, and shame. I admitted that I had lived recklessly, and that I no longer wanted to run the show. I had made a mess of things and finally asked for help, and meant it.

I was getting the hang of this fear thing. You must learn to live not without fear, but without the FEAR that paralyzes. Whatever you fear more than closing your heart will forever keep you from your full awakening. We must cultivate a vastness of Inner Presence that embraces our fears. It is then that we become courageous. That Inner Presence is our *loveseed*.

It's the same with anger. Without it, you let people run over you. Anger tells you when a boundary has been crossed and how to draw a line in the sand. When you feel it fully, you activate a great power, and much of the time you do not even need to draw the line, because people respect you for being real. You can do it all with love.

And then there is sadness, grief. Ah, grief. It connects you with the fabric of humanity in the most reverent way. Krishnamurti once said, "It is no measure of health to be well adjusted to a profoundly sick society." Maybe feeling your grief is exactly what you need to be whole and happy.

The shadow of this full-spectrum living is the bipolarity of most people's lives. You forget the design, the pulse of living, and find yourself out of step on the far edges of life, removed from your center, busy avoiding the pain that is the doorway to your own freedom. You feel caught and blame it on your chemistry. In *The Untethered Soul*, author Michael Singer says, "Spiritual growth exists in that moment when you are consciously willing to pay the price of freedom. You must be willing at all times and in all circumstances, to remain conscious in the face of pain and to work with your heart by relaxing and remaining open."

I promise that if you can learn to feel whatever emotion is present, knowing that it is the way to connect to your *loveseed*, you will live a meaningful life with a large measure of joy and for most of you, without medication.

The power of pure intention

Full-spectrum living involves active intent. I ask you to use your imaginal faculties to see intention as a form of love. Love as intention. Love as command, not request. You are steering the ship, and you command with intention. Love as intention. If you are out of harmony with yourself or the world, you will notice that you failed to set a clear intention.

You can set micro intentions for your days, but it is wise for you to set an overall intention for your life at this time. Take it to the highest level that feels real for you right now. I suggest reaching for a very powerful archetypal energy and merging it with what you presently have available in your awareness. For example, you can set the intention to tap into the Way-Shower Archetype. (Variations would be Sage, Wise Man or Woman, Elder.) You can decide that every time you lose your way, you show a path to other beings who feel lost and attribute the highest level of intention to everything that unfolds.

Intention is the meaning you give to the unfolding of your life. It is entirely subjective, and there is no inherent meaning other than what you give to it. Meaning becomes your intentional perception, as well as a vibrational experience in the body. Intention helps you co-create without having to focus on a particular outcome. When you set your intention high, you raise your vibration and adopt a wider view.

Remember that since we are made up of energy and the level at which we are vibrating influences outcome, to make a change we would need to shift the inner vibration, which arises from our emotions. The emotions you experience throughout a given day are the energy level at which you are vibrating. In order to create prosperity, love, happiness, or anything in your outer world, you must feel your way to the higher emotional vibration. A true master can choose the one point that will create the shift.

Intention has nothing to do with control and everything to do with command. You deliberately attribute higher meanings to the activities you engage in every day. Some examples are:

"With every bite I eat, I become a stronger vessel for Spirit and an agent of gratitude on the planet."

"With every dollar I spend, I gratefully contribute to the free flowing of infinite prosperity on the planet."

"With every child I teach, I feel the joy of becoming a force for the full awakening of humanity."

"With every bit of darkness I face in myself, I courageously clear the path for others to know their light."

This sets intention to contribute to outcomes from the highest aspect of your Divine self. It allows you to move from the cave of the heart to the mountain of the mind— the very highest view you can take of your life. According to the Master Abraham, who is channeled by Esther Hicks, if you can hold a simple thought or intention for 17 seconds without contradicting it, another thought that is vibrationally like it will be attracted to it. At precisely the 17-second point, these two thoughts will join one another and coalesce and become a bigger and more evolved and faster vibrating thought. When that happens, energy is expended. It is like a combustion point, and energy or interest begins to bubble up in the person having the thought.

If you can stay focused on this topic that you have chosen for another 17 seconds, at the moment you cross the 34-second mark (2 x 17), another, more-evolved thought will be attracted to it, and these two more evolved thoughts coalesce and there is another combustion point. At that point, these two thoughts become one, higher and faster in vibration.

If you can maintain your attention to that now more evolved thought, at the 51-second mark (3 x 17) there is yet another coalescing, another joining of thought and another combustion point.

If you can hold that more evolved thought for another 17 seconds, the same thing happens, and when you cross the 68-second mark, you have a combustion big enough to affect physical manifestation.

Abraham says that 17 seconds of pure thought is equivalent to 2,000 hours of action. If you can cross the 34-second mark, you can multiply your action by ten, equaling 20,000 action-hours. If you can cross the 51-second mark (3 x 17), you can multiply by ten again, a 200,000 action-hour equivalent. If you can cross the 68-second mark—just over a minute of pure undiluted thought—it is equivalent to more than two million action-hours.

This is a remarkable way to leverage thought, and yet, we are less able to do this than ever, as there are forces preventing people from having pure focused thought on the highest good—one of them being the addiction to electronic devices. According to Abraham, the average person begins contradicting their pure thought after eight seconds, which explains a lot. Understand that the reverse is also true. When you hold a negative thought for longer than 68 seconds, you can see how it manifests in your reality and how it programs your DNA to think that is the way it is, encoding the psyche with limited vision. Thankfully we cannot maintain unobstructed focus on a negative thought very easily, either. If your life isn't what you want, you are stronger in the ability to maintain what you don't want. Take a look as *Compassionate Witness* and you'll see it clearly.

Counter intentions

Our negative thoughts are our counter intentions, which are part of our shadow. They are the fears we harbor inside that the false self doesn't want to face. There was a time of innocence when we did not have them. We are often not aware of them, but if we consciously name and face them, we take away the power they have over us and we enter into a new state free from fear, returning us to the original state of innocence, this time with consciousness.

This alchemical work is based on the Universal Law of Polarity, which states that everything can be separated into two completely opposite parts and that within each of them the other is contained. This is another way of speaking about wave particle duality, which is part of the plan of Creation. In other words, particles have the potentiality of waves, waves have the potentiality of particles, white has black, yin has yang, low exists with high, slow is also fast, elation exists with depression, kindness exists with cruelty, generosity exists alongside greed, and on and on it goes on planet Earth.

If you think about the way children experience life, they don't label these things. They simply experience them in their raw and unabridged and unedited form. There is not yet a cognitive process to construct beliefs and shoulds. If they are hungry, they cry, and then easily shift to contentment if they are fed. If they are frightened by a loud noise, they will startle and cry to release the stress, but as soon as they are comforted, they settle down again.

But as we become educated in the ways of the family and the culture and our personalities form around the need to be accepted, we stop crying when we are hungry or frightened, and the mind takes over to attempt to keep us safe. The mind begins to comment constantly and to worry about the self. It attempts to be certain, get it right, and solve problems, and even becomes addicted to this task. If a child has been starved of physical food or emotional comfort, the mind will take over to solve that problem, which may lead to issues with food or relationships. It seeks to create external changes that don't get to the root of the problem, which is the fear in the mind itself—the fear of not having enough food or love. It is a pernicious form of suffering that begins to control and dull our lives. It creates massive anxiety, for the mind cannot figure it all out, let alone control it. It's not the mind's job, but it's very hard to convince the mind of that!

Getting back to physics, it has been observed in laboratories that when you collide a positively-charged electron and also the electron's anti-particle with a negatively-charged particle, there is an explosion, both are annihilated, and out of that destruction gamma-ray photons—light—are created. When positive and negative come together, they birth light, which is an expression of love. This happens in the *Zero Point* field of the heart—also known as Implicate Order—you learned about in Chapter 4.

Everything that is and ever will be is enfolded within the Implicate Order. There is a special cosmic movement that carries forth the process of enfoldment and unfoldment into the explicate order or material world. When we align our minds with this cosmic movement, allowing the Universe to give us endless feedback to which we can respond with innocence, we open to endless possibility.

When applied to your emotions, when you take a negative emotion and identify the equal and opposite positive emotion that coexists alongside it, the negative emotion is annihilated and you open to love. This is something the mind can do! It wants to do something, so show it how to create an explosion of love in your heart.

For example, when your husband cheats on you and you initially see the event as tragic, as my client Tanya did, you will, of course, experience sadness, anger, jealousy, doubt, depression, and fear. The mind will tell you that something is wrong, and you cannot fight the mind, because you will always lose. The mind is sure that these feelings are not good and may convince you to see a therapist or psychiatrist. If that helping professional is afraid that you will become overwhelmed with those emotions and does not know how to help you move them due to lack of skill or fear, he or she may convince you to take an anti-depressant and or anti-anxiety medication. It happens all the time.

But if you stop and *Witness* your emotions, feeling and naming them and the story attached to them—*I am feeling sad because I planned to remain married forever and now he is gone and with another woman because I am unlovable*—if you fully feel all of it, you will naturally begin to shift. By naming the feelings, you activate the neo-cortex, which is the thinking part of the brain, and there is a top-down feedback loop that informs your limbic or emotional system about what is being experienced. We acknowledge our suffering, which lays the groundwork for compassion. We move back into the cave of the heart again.

By surrendering resistance to the feelings, you will begin to see the ways in which he was possibly controlling and unkind, and now that he is gone, you can live your life without having to shrink yourself and feel hurt much of the time. Maybe he was a stick in the mud, and now you are going places and meeting people you never would have if he had not left you.

In other words, for every reason that you feel sad, there is going to be a reason to also be happy, if you allow it. Every time you allow yourself to fully feel an emotion, you create the equal experience of the opposite. This allowing perspective opens the doorway to seeing the world as it truly is; the play of opposites in the ever-jiggling dance of life. As you allow yourself to perceive both sides simultaneously, you open yourself to the divine perfection of the Universe, whose purpose is equilibrium and synchronicity.

Our brains construct our reality by interpreting frequencies from other dimensions, and the main stress that keeps us from reaching higher frequencies comes from our suppressed and repressed emotions as the mind attempts to solve matters on the outside. The frantic mind becomes the wise *Witness* when we soften the heart so that there can be a gentle looping between the mind and the heart. It is the way to find the child inside who carries the highest vision.

Have you ever been warned to "manage your expectations"? It's a good idea when it comes to many things in the world of form, but it limits us in the realm of Spirit. The popular Christian preacher Joel Osteen reminds us to "wait with expectancy," as the countless Old and New Testament teachings declare, and this thinking is aligned with the Universal Laws of Attraction.

In a sense, to "wait with expectancy" is a step beyond belief in the realm of knowing. That is the innocent mindset that the *Path of Zero* guides you toward. It is a dimension beyond doubt, in the realm of deep faith. It is what Rumi meant when he said, "Sell your cleverness and buy bewilderment." It is what the great writer and philosopher Aldous Huxley meant when he said, "Sit down before fact as a little child, be prepared to give up every preconceived notion, follow humbly wherever and to whatever abysses nature leads, or you shall learn nothing."

Further decoding

Setting your intent is one thing, yet often there is trauma locked in your nervous system, and your reaction to this is part of the problem, but you focus on the symptoms as do doctors. There are other ways to become free, and doing the inner work of re-consolidating traumatic memories can be done in several ways, often with the assistance of healers of the body, mind, and heart.

Thoughts create emotions and emotions create thoughts. Chemicals create emotions and emotions create chemicals. Thoughts create emotions that create chemicals and negative thoughts completely change the processing of neurotransmitters in the body. **Expressing emotion is an electrochemical event that allows a system to remain healthy. One of the main causes of disease is suppressing emotion, which causes the voltage to drop.**

I am sure there are many who dispute this and who adhere to the idea of the chemical imbalance to explain the increasing number of expressions of emotional dysregulation we have today. The root cause of the dysfunction is within your vibrational field first, and that is where the deeper healing takes place. Not only do old limiting beliefs exert their affect by creating an electromagnetic charge within the person, but it has been discovered that the charge can exist in the electromagnetic field around the body.

The groundbreaking work of Eileen McKusick called Biofield Tuning has shown us that we may contain many "charged" vibrations from unexpressed emotion in the vibrational field around the body, in what is called plasma, which is the fourth state of matter (liquid, solid, gas, plasma), and which she calls the *biofield.* Eileen is a pioneer in a new understanding of the electric nature of the Universe. She has mapped out the field showing us that the many emotions and emotional states, as well as physical illnesses that we suffer from, are related to charges that are "stuck" in a person's electromagnetic field. Tuning forks can be used to break up the charge and in essence, clear the person's energy field that may have even held a charge passed down from one's ancestors. I believe that tuning forks and other such "vibrational medicine" are the healing tools we need for the so-called "mental illness" of our times, far more than the endless variety of psycho-pharmaceuticals that offer the quick fix, yet always with side effects.

Regardless of circumstance, an action you can always take is to use your breath to return to your own vibration, for your breath is always your own. Your own natural breath is a river that leads back to Source, to God. It is available all the time, and when you put your attention on the breath, you immediately become more present and more conscious.

What creates the great despair in modern life is not the vast freedom and plethora of choices, but the fact that we are paralyzed in our resistance; our fear for which we create new excuses, new illnesses and new drugs. Let the resistance simply be a part of the journey. Be bigger than the resistance, the fear, the excuses, and know that Love is the great power.

The persona is the mask that conceals the *True Self* and includes your personality—the part of you separated from essence. Your *Soul* has unique attributes—a kind of signature flavor. The more it shines through your personality, the wiser and more compassionate you become. *Spirit* is pure consciousness, infinite and indivisible, and from whence we all came. The further away from Spirit you live your life, the more bipolar your experience will be; the more likely it will be that you get caught in an addiction that sidetracks you from realizing your true magnificence. Remember, we are always drawn back to Source, which is Spirit, and the Soul is the bridge back.

Beyond attachment

When we repress and bury hurt, we repress our longing for God as well, and the longing comes out in a distorted way. Addiction uses up our natural desire and replaces love with pale substitutes. Instead of Spirit, you crave spirits. Instead of nurturance, you crave the sweetness of sugar—the return to the womb that heroin simulates. If our ecstasy is anything less than God's angel, we are wise to never surrender to it.

We have been given free will, and there is a force in each of us which guides us "home" to our *loveseed* if we can surrender our will to that force. We must choose freely, without coercion or manipulation, to love God, Self, and others as the deepest desire of our hearts. Then we are free, no matter how we may be caught in the moment.

Forget willpower altogether. As soon you attempt to control a truly addictive behavior by making resolutions from your will, you begin to defeat yourself, because there is always a mixed motivation. One part of you may sincerely want to be free, while your inner Addict is attached to the addictive behavior which is much stronger. Addiction splits the will in two, and this internal inconsistency zaps our confidence and self-respect. How can we feel confident if we don't really know what we want? Most of our pain is due to lack of a deeper truth. When you are caught in conflict, the opposite of pain is not pleasure, but clarity.

The Buddhist term for addiction or craving means "unquenchable thirst." This craving is natural, particularly if the *loveseed* has not been watered. One of the hallmarks of addiction is the inability to stop the connection with the addictive behavior or substance. Because of inner psychic pain, the person clings to what helps make the pain go away, even if only temporarily.

The object of our addiction competes for our attention, and for love to be fully actualized our attention must be free. You must ask for help from a Higher Power to guide you in your singular intention to become free, even as the Addict part of you continues to win over and over. If you continue to set your sails on freedom, even while you are "hooked," you are heading toward freedom. Never forget that. The Addict comes along for the ride.

Many teachers are saying very similar things because there is actually a way that is both universal, and simultaneously, unique to each person. Maybe you need accountability in a 12-Step Program to help you detach and reinforce new ways of living. See what you can do, beginning with setting a clear intention and sticking with it.

Practice is key, as is working with the lighter issues first, as you would with lighter weights if you want to strength-train with weights. You really do build emotional and spiritual muscles and create new wiring in your brain. It is personal psychic surgery that frees up so much energy to create and enjoy your life, rather than feeding the Addict.

Recovery is getting to the place beyond attachment. It is getting to the truth of who you are. It is only when you lovingly stop and caress the wild urge welling up from the depths of you to drink, smoke, fuck, work, or shop that you begin to make friends with the very energy that you were about to overlook. This part of you is not civilized. It lives outside the acceptable parameters of consensus and is uniquely you. Everything else is an imitation. When you can stand naked with that part of you fully seen, fully open, and fully awake, the magic you sought in champagne or chocolate or cocaine is your very own to offer your life, to offer life itself.

Fueling all addiction is the ache that comes from being disconnected from our *loveseed*. You must feel that ache, which is often experienced as a great emptiness; a hollowness that you will want to fill or make go away.

That very emptiness is where Grace can enter; where the Universe can live inside you.

If you are caught in an addiction right now, whether to a substance, a process, or a person, begin to reflect on these things, remembering that you are preparing the ground for love. Be clear that when you source from anything other than Source, you are still caught. Keep a prayer in your heart, a vow that you will eventually fulfill, no matter how many times you disappoint yourself by attempting to use willpower.

Know that surrender is your friend when it comes to any addiction, and getting help is the beginning of that process. Each time you surrender, you experience a mystic death of your ego, which is part of being fully human. Surrendering often involves a kind of forgiveness, where you release the meaning you have made of something. You let go of the meaning and the need to be right because it binds you to the downward pull.

Our attachment is to the meaning we have made of everything. That is all there is to be attached to—our interpretation of what is happening. Once you surrender your attachment to the meaning, you are able to see what is really happening from a much more expansive point of view and you are ready for true healing. You no longer have to use that energy to hide yourself, which is a wonderful gift to the world.

You begin to heal your relationship with time, as well. Rather than thinking in terms of time—how much you've lost, how fast it's moving, how little you have left—you begin to think in terms of expansion. The best reason to get free of an addiction is the awesome aliveness that comes from infinitely expanding into the moment, because you are so present.

True healing

True healing is when you see the opportunity for growth that a painful situation has provided. We realize that we don't have to fix ourselves, because we are not broken. In fact, all self-improvement is just an investment in an old way of thinking. Geneen Roth says in her book *When Food Is Love*, "The purpose of healing is not to be forever happy; that is impossible. The purpose of healing is to be awake. And to live while you are alive instead of dying while you are alive. Healing is about being broken and whole at the same time. Healing is about opening our hearts, not closing them. It is about softening the places in us that won't let love in. Healing is a process."

It is important to distinguish between healing and curing. Curing is the business of medicine and has to do with eliminating symptoms, but seldom results in a healing. Healing is an entirely different proposition and works on several levels at once: the energetic or vibrational, the level of the soul or mythic level, the psychological where you shift beliefs, and the actual where you engage in new behaviors, and adopt new diets, do yoga, meditate, and so on.

We need to go for Quantum Healing now, because we are multidimensional beings. The *Hero's Journey* of today may involve the residue from past lives, for as you recall, time is not linear. All is not happening now, but all exists now.

The pain of losing a child in a past life can lead to struggle in this life that is not understood on the psychological level alone, which is why there are limits to most psychotherapy.

Illness often arises when your soul evolves faster than your body can keep up with, and getting sick gives permission for your body to rest and slow things down so deeper healing can happen.

One of the most beautiful stories of healing happened early in my career as a psychotherapist, when I was directing several psychodrama groups at a psychiatric hospital. There was a man named Joe on the unit who had attempted suicide and who was totally resistant to the medications prescribed to "cure" his deep depression. He had a leg amputated at the knee and an arm amputated at the elbow due to a nearly fatal accident. Indeed, the real source of his depression was that he longed to express the woman inside him, whom he called JoAnn. This was in 1991, long before Bruce Jenner and many others brought the issue of transgenderism into public awareness.

Joe was married to a woman he loved deeply, and he had four young daughters. He had no desire to leave his wife, nor to have surgery, but merely wanted to cross-dress. He told the story of how he felt transported to a much happier world when he put stockings on his prosthetic leg.

That afternoon on the psychiatric unit, Joe was chosen to be the protagonist in the psychodrama I was directing. I began by asking him when in his life he had felt the happy feeling he has when he cross-dresses. Joe was in his wheelchair that day, and as he closed his eyes, he told the story of being with his two sisters who used to dress him up with all their prettiest clothing. I could see a change come over his face, and I asked him to choose two people to play his sisters. As Joe talked about what was happening back in his childhood with his sisters, the two women began to delicately drape the sheer scarves from my huge bag over Joe's head and shoulders, intuitively knowing what to say.

The group was riveted as a huge ray of sunlight poured into the room radiating Joe's beatific face. Joe grew up in an alcoholic family with a dearth of warmth, play, and love. The only time he felt truly cared for and happy were the few times his sisters included him in their magical world. This was when he was most connected to his *loveseed*, so he naturally longed for any semblance of that sweet energy.

When Joe left the hospital, he and his devoted wife June began working with me as a couple. I smile, as I had little to no training in working with couples at that point, but my fierce belief in the power of healing carried the work. We let JoAnn, Joe's inner woman, be fully present in the sessions, and June got to know her better. Her fears about their children were allayed as Joe promised to keep his need for cross-dressing completely sacred and separate from them.

June was a devout Catholic and wondered about the "rightness" of such behavior. I knew in my heart of hearts that if June attempted to make Joe eliminate the cross-dressing all together, Joe was so fragile that he could make another suicide attempt. I basically told her that her acceptance of Joe as he is, with the limits in place, was the greatest gift of love that she could offer him, and that, eventually, they would find their way with everything if Joe kept to his promise.

June and Joe worked hard, and June and JoAnn became good friends. June actually began to see the beauty in her husband as he developed this nurturing, feminine nature even more with her and their children. She joked that JoAnn did a far better job than she did getting snarls out of the girls' hair. Joe's lightness of spirit began to return, something neither of them had experienced in years.

They eventually moved across the country, and because it was pre-internet, we did not keep in contact, until one day many years later I received a postcard from June:

> Dear Kathleen,
>
> We've lived in San Diego for several years, and Laura is already about to go off the college. All the kids are doing great, and Joe and I are very happy. We just kept accepting JoAnn, and eventually, Joe didn't feel the need to cross-dress any more. We really thank you for helping us all those years ago.

Admittedly, receiving that postcard made my day, not because Joe was no longer cross-dressing, which was not the point. He had reclaimed his life and their family was thriving. Acceptance is a precious gift!

Getting on with things

When I returned to Northern Virginia per order of the powers-that-be, I lived in my sister's basement for six months. Her husband Frank joked that it was "The Home for Wayward Hanagans," as others in the family had spent time in the expansive and cozy basement. I built a garden for Peggy and Frank as a way of expressing gratitude, for I truly had no money by the time I arrived, and I knew that digging in the earth would "ground my ass," as my friend Rose would say.

In stark contrast to the slamming doors of Portland, I found that settling in Del Ray, a little village four miles from Washington, D.C. in the city of Alexandria, opened doors, and soon I had both former and new clients whom I could guide. One step led to the next, and before long I was settled enough to feel the urge in my heart brimming over to write this book.

In that time, I remember crying really big; my heart was brimming over with gratitude—to my sister and her husband, to my mother, to the landlord who rented me my office for dirt-cheap for the first four months because I shared with him that I was beginning again after a tough time. I would not have done that before, but I had learned a few things in the course of losing everything. I remembered my friend Chris who talked me out of declaring bankruptcy, and the gals who let me live with them for very cheap so I could make it. I felt the breath of a choir of angels at my back.

No one acts alone. No one can act alone. In fact, trying to do it all alone is a setup. We are acting in cooperation with many others, living in parallel Universes, each in our own, coming together as divine sparks to bring this stage of the bigger plan for humanity to fruition—the awakening of our Sacred Hearts. It has, in fact, already happened, and each time you have a moment of deep gratitude, you stop competing with the Universe or whatever you call that bigger energy. You say, "Bring it on. Bring on the help. Bring on the support. I am ready to receive."

I learned that handing over my will was the best thing I could do to get things to happen along the lines of my dream and my destiny. I had lived out some heavy karmic energy and somehow, through it all, I was awake enough to realize what was happening. I was ready to shift.

My very own life had become my mother and father, my guru, and my smartest professor, mirroring back to me all I needed to know to course-correct. I had developed a trust in life that goes beyond proof and beyond the need to be seen and validated—a deep trust in my own life. When you are able to surrender the need to be validated, you begin to develop the trust of knowing. This knowing is of the heart, and you must pay attention to this knowing so you do not fall into doubt and become easily misguided.

If you recall from the diagram of the *Hero's Journey*, after being in the belly of the beast the hero meets allies and teachers and finally has a breakthrough and brings back a gift, often called an *elixir*, leading to a kind of celebration.

One of the teachers I met along the way is a marvelous man named Mooji. From *Breath of the Absolute*, his words now ring true for me, in the most authentic way: "The fear is always greater than the actuality. The fear comes because of lack of trust. You feel you can take better care of yourself than God can. You fear what God may have planned for you may not be what you want. This is probably true because the dreams we have are confined to what we know of life and ourselves, which is infinitesimal to the vastness that is. When we let go of what we think will make us happy, we allow Grace to breathe, and great and beautiful things not even imagined of are given space to happen.

I came into this knowing, and I knew I still had much light to share. In fact, I was just now getting started as I moved from living my karma to living my dharma.

CHAPTER 11

From Karma to Dharma

"True mastery, authentic dharma,
is not possible without the kernel of the
Gift at the center of the false self."
– Stephen Cope

Living your dharma

I invite you to consider that the plan that the Universe/ God/Spirit, has for you is far more vast than your local, fear-based ego could ever imagine. It may not have anything to do with a solid retirement plan, and yet, the failure to fulfill that "higher" plan could leave you with a deep sense of unease. In fact, the following quote from the Gospel of Thomas, Verse 70, expresses a deep, all-pervasive truth for most human beings: "If you bring forth what is within you, what you bring forth will save you. If you do not bring forth what is within you, what you do not bring forth will destroy you."

At one time that sounded so ominous to me, and now I want to share from a perspective of possibility that says you are never far from your true self, and thus never far from bringing forth what is within you. It's so close you could trip over it, or minimize its impact. And yet, we all long to know our sacred reason for being here.

In Chapter Four, you learned that *Zero Point*, located in the center of your chest, is also inextricably connected to your personal heart and to your life's calling—that which you are here to manifest as only you can. There truly is a heartache when we hear that call and refuse to heed it. We block the spiritual energy that would be released if we did. When you do connect to this spiritual energy, you connect to yet another heart, a bigger intelligence—the *Global Heart*—and begin to feel the pain of the world. The call is the call to find your way of flowing infinite love toward the world—toward all of life. You become intimate with all things—with life itself. You become sovereign, and a mighty force of good, in your own way.

The American poet and theologian Frederick Buechner says, "Where our deep gladness and the world's hunger meet, we hear a further call." When you heed that call, you are fulfilling your *dharma*. If you look at the Venn diagram below, there is a place where the world's need, your joy, and your gift all come together—the "sweet spot" of your dharma.

Coming to know and embrace that sweet spot is the journey of a lifetime, and many people struggle in a big way with doing so. Being able to "make a living" is also a reality we must reckon with, and the ideal would look something like the "sweet spot" in the center of the diagram below. To bring the gift and the joy to what is needed in the world, and make a living from what you receive, is a blessing beyond all blessings and is far from the norm in our present culture. Though it can certainly be done within a traditional structure, many people become entrepreneurs and artists to realize this. At the center is an aliveness that contributes to a new and vibrant culture of prosperity.

Though you may make money fulfilling your *dharma*, it is in living your *dharma* that a holy channel is opened up for all kinds of prosperity to enter, including money if that is what is desired. This is key: you must decide to receive it, but when you seek only money, you forfeit dharma.

Dharma is a key concept with multiple meanings. In western languages there is no single-word translation for *dharma*, and yet it points to your essential nature. The word closest in meaning in English is *purpose*, which has a typically western spin on its meaning as something outside of you that you must find and make money doing.

In recent years, purpose has become something that people are willing to pay someone thousands of dollars to help them find, but like the fellow who lost his keys a few miles back and looks for them under the street lamp down the road because the light is brighter, it is unlikely that anyone will find their purpose that way. Your *dharma* has been with you all along, and it is an expression of your *loveseed*."

In Hinduism, *dharma* signifies the behaviors that are considered to be in alignment with the order of the Universe— a kind of right way of living. In Buddhism, *dharma* means cosmic law and order, and also applies to the teachings of the Buddha, which were based on cosmic law and order.

Many indigenous societies believe that we all possess *original medicine* a kind of personal power that is ours and ours alone. It is true that no two people possess the exact combination of strengths, talents, and challenges. This means that if we compare ourselves to others, we are disowning our *original medicine*. If our *medicine* is the gift we bring to the world, then not believing in ourselves and our unique *medicine* affects everyone.

Emanating from our *loveseed*—our priceless and incomparable *original medicine*—is often not valued in a world where we are taught to compare and compete. In fact, it may not even be recognized. In her book *Transformational Speaking,* Gail Larsen says, "We are often unaware of our medicine or devalue it because our inherent gifts come naturally to us. What is natural is effortless, so it can seem 'ordinary.' We can also obscure our medicine by pursuing directions that are not aligned with who we really are and who we are here to be." So you can see that dynamic in action, I have shared with you the devastation to my health and finances when I pursued that which was not mine to claim.

When you commit to finding and living your *original medicine*, you are on the path of your *dharma*. You throw away the yardsticks from "the authorities" or aspects of the culture that keep you tethered to old molds that have nothing to do with you or what the world needs now. There is enormous freedom when you refuse to measure yourself against others, and there is joy and pleasure in seeing the spark of *original medicine* in everyone and everything. That is living your *dharma*.

I say that dharma is what we teach by our actions. It goes beyond us, and I recommend letting your dharma be as powerful as you can possibly express it. Karma, on the other hand, is considered in Hinduism and Buddhism to be the sum of a person's actions in this and previous states of existence, or what Westerners refer to as fate. This points to our suffering and fears, whereas *dharma* points to what we express on the other side of our suffering and fears. Real spirituality is when we allow our sorrows to teach us the way we are meant to serve. You are being led by your Soul. There is nothing better, really. When you are living your *dharma*, you essentially live according to the highest law, which is love. You are fulfilling the highest expression of yourself. You are fully who you are, expressing your *essence*, your *loveseed*. You could say that your *dharma* has the same relationship to you as sweetness does to sugar. They are inseparable.

You could say that your *dharma* is expressed in the "sweet spot" where what you have been given, your fate, meets free will, which is what you do with it. To live your *dharma* you must exercise your sovereign free will, which means you take full responsibility for every facet of your life. This means you have ultimate power.

To do that, you must connect to the one power that is the source of all power. That is the real meaning of sovereignty, which points to the King and Queen archetypes. The King and Queen were originally thought to receive their power directly from God, according to the medieval political doctrine called the divine right of kings. To live your *dharma* you claim your divine right. When we activate the energy of these archetypes consciously, we take back the power we lost to the conditioning we've been immersed in since birth.

Sovereignty lies in the choices we make day-to-day. It is a capacity and quality of your Soul inherent in who you are. The source of your sovereignty is your *loveseed,* and you can see how much it is related to your *dharma.* It's as if we each have a manifesto inside—the insistent urge of the Divine to express itself through us.

If you are human, you have been called. The only answer that will fulfill you is YES. And you must express yourself. You must take a stand for something, or you will fall for what is not real, get caught in shoulds and rules of the culture, and remain blind to your own greatness. To fulfill your *dharma,* you must become a messenger of love. By being fully who you are, you contribute to oneness on the planet.

This is what I have asked of you

I witnessed this in the most touching and profound way when I lived in Massachusetts. In trying to find my tribe, I discovered a spiritually-oriented wellness center. On one of the days I visited, there was much excitement in the air about a spiritual teacher named Juelle, visiting from another community. I was told that Juelle channels the Ascended Masters, the beings of Light who live in a higher dimension and always have the best interest of humanity at heart. When I heard she was hosting a group gathering, I thought about my mother, and trusted my intuition to ask if she would like to attend. At 81, she was game!

When we arrived, the usual social introductions followed, and we took our seats in the small room of about 25 people. Juelle was "down home" and very warm and engaging. When she shifted into channeling the Masters, she spoke no differently than she did when being herself, other than more intensely, in an effort to reach into the hearts of everyone present. She was living her *dharma*, full out. You can read about her in her book called *Walk-In* by Juelle.

She asked the group, "Do you know why you are not fulfilling the big dreams in your hearts? Do you know why you haven't written that book or left that job or that abusive relationship? Do you know why you haven't gotten that invention patented that could help people? Do you know why? It's not because you are not capable or you don't deserve it, but because you have been programmed to believe that you cannot or should not.

You have been taught lies by people who could not see who you truly are, and who fed you ideas of limitation and lack. It's not your fault, and it's not theirs. This was done to them. The real reason you have not realized how magnificent you truly are is because you have been deeply hurt by these lies. And yet, there is someone in this room, who, if they touched your heart, lifetimes of shame and fear would drop away, and you would be seen for who you truly are."

Juelle then turned to my mother and attuned to her discomfort. My mother had never been public about her gift, though our family and anyone who knew her had been blessed by her gift of deep acceptance, which is her *dharma*.

There was a gentle back and forth between Juelle and Mom, and finally Juelle asked her to get up and go to each person and simply see them and touch them with her acceptance. My mother hesitated. She said, "I've only ever done that in my family." Juelle said, "This is your family. We are all one family." Mom understood.

As my mother went to each person, I witnessed the most sacred transmission. She first went to a young woman in the back of the room. Mom hugged her saying, "I came to you first because you need it the most. You need to feel loved." As Mom held her, the young woman broke down, saying, "My mother never loved me and I was raised by my father and he just died, and I have no one." This continued until each person had been seen. My heart burst with awe, pride, and joy.

On the ride home, I asked my mother what that experience was like for her. She said she had never realized she could do that with others, because she had been so busy doing what she could for her own large family. I asked her how she arrived at the ability to be so accepting of herself, others, and life in general. She said something I already knew, which was that living with my fiercely-loving and very difficult father was the main teacher, and then each of us, her seven children.

She reflected on a moment when she fully realized what her purpose in life truly was. It was when we were all actively involved in school and activities and she turned the family station wagon into a school bus to make extra money. She was exhausted, money was tight, and every day was the same—more and more work, more and more output, and more and more ways she was not sure she was doing a good job.

She said she felt so defeated that day, and in her exhaustion all she knew to do was to pray. She asked God to help her understand what her purpose was and if she was doing what He wanted. She said God spoke to her saying, "Peggy, you are raising seven good human beings who will go on to make the world a better place. You are doing a very good job, and this is what I have asked of you. This is your purpose." And it was, and still is, now with the grandchildren and a great grandchild. It continues on and on, and the effects of her love and acceptance ripple out in huge waves in her own immediate family and beyond. It is rippling to you right now as you read this.

When you realize that you are living your *dharma*, you often think "How did I miss this? I was looking here and there, and all the time I was living my dharma." If that happens, you are blessed.

Dharma and the wounded healer

Healing and *dharma* are intimately related. As I have said in earlier chapters, there is a connection between the gift and the wound. The archetype of the *wounded healer* is a term created by Carl Jung that says the therapist is compelled to treat patients because the therapist himself or herself is "wounded." It is believed that the idea has Greek mythological origins, as the pattern or archetype of the *wounded healer* can be seen over and over again throughout the history of humanity and is still relevant today.

Chiron was a centaur and was known as a wise teacher, healer, and prophet. His father was the Greek god Kronus, and his mother was a beautiful nymph named Philyra. Kronus was a cruel and devouring father-god who, when he met the nymph, decided to dominate her sexually. Philyra had no attraction to the lusty Kronus, so she turned herself into a mare in the attempt to flee his unwelcome desirous advances. Likewise, Kronus transformed himself into a stallion, forcing himself on Philyra, then left, never to return.

Upon seeing her newborn son, Chiron, clearly a centaur, Philyra is disgusted and appalled, rejecting and abandoning him. This is Chiron's first wounding, and I have witnessed this very pattern more than I could ever have imagined before becoming a psychotherapist. The good news is that Chiron is later adopted by the Greek sun god Apollo, the god of music, prophecy, poetry, and healing. Apollo taught Chiron all he knew, and as a result, Chiron became a powerful mentor to the sons of kings and Greek heroes such as Achilles and Hercules.

During a skirmish with a rowdy crowd of centaurs, Hercules carelessly and accidentally wounded his friend and mentor Chiron in the knee with one of his arrows. The arrow he used was coated with the blood of the Hydra monster, which was known to cause painful wounds that never heal. This was Chiron's second wounding.

Because Chiron was immortal, having a wound that would never heal was a serious matter, as he could never heal and never die. This is karma at its most brutal. How many of you have felt that way? The only way you could get relief is to die, but the God in you will not let you simply die, for that part of you is immortal.

As time went on, being unable to heal himself with his herbs and brews though able to heal others, Chiron suffered a great deal.

When Hercules released Prometheus, whom Zeus had imprisoned for giving the gift of fire to man, Chiron willingly gave up his life and consented to die in Prometheus' place. This kind centaur renounced immortality, taught man the art of medicine, reared many famous disciples, and was a man of great justice, conscientiousness, and diligence. As a way to honor him, Chiron was immortalized after his death and given a place amongst the stars in the constellation Centaurus.

Chiron embodies the spirit of compassion and selfless service that all healers must possess. His agonizing wound symbolizes the transformative power of illness and suffering and shows us that when we bring consciousness to our personal wounds, both psychic and physical, we can become sources of great moral and spiritual strength for others.

In Steven Cope's *The Great Work of Your Life* he says, "Dharma calls us not to just any old battlefield, but to the battlefield where we will suffer most fruitfully. Where our suffering will be most useful to ourselves, our work, and to the world." It is beautiful; the treasure hunt for the gift at the center of your wound. It gives your life an elevated sense of meaning and purpose, particularly the difficult parts.

In the case of my mother, her first significant wounding was the day the telegram arrived during World War II. My mother was 14 years old, the youngest of three. Her hero in so many ways, her older brother Billy was on a naval ship in the South Pacific. My mother answered the door to receive a telegram, saw the three stars that meant Billy had been killed, then had to deliver that message to my grandmother.

When she told me the story, she said, "It was the day I grew up. I saw my mother fall to the floor, screaming and in such pain. Then, one after the other, I watched my father and other family members come home and get the news. I saw their reactions, and it attuned me to other people's pain." On that day, my mother's innocence was replaced with an inconsolable grief. She did not show her grief to the world, but instead showed the love that was behind it. That is *dharma*.

That connection to our grief is key to realizing our *dharma*. I don't mean it in a tragic sense. My mother is one of the most positive and optimistic people you would ever meet. She just knows that place of pain and carries on in spite of it, and yet is not disconnected from it, nor from Joy. Our *dharma* teaches us to evolve by requiring that we let go of the small self for the sake of a greater Self.

Where fate meets free will

One of the most poignant examples of the wounded healer and living one's *dharma* can be seen in the life of the 14th Lama.

Lhamo Thondup was born on July 6, 1935, in a remote village in northeastern Tibet. He was the fifth of the seven surviving children of his mother, who lost nine of her 16 children in infancy. The family farmed buckwheat and barley and raised livestock. He lived close to his mother—a happy child in a loving family, but not for long. When the 13th Dalai Lama died in 1933, three search parties were sent out to find the child whom they would recognize as his reincarnation.

Through visions and following signs, they were led to the small farmhouse where Lhamo lived. When the head of the search party disguised himself as a servant so he could interact with the baby Dalai Lama, he saw that the child, only two years old, knew who he was. A larger group of dignitaries descended upon the child's home to observe, and soon declared that the 14th Dalai Lama had been found.

Lhamo was separated from his parents and began his training to become one of the most influential and kindest spiritual leaders of all time. This was the first wounding. On February 22, 1940, at the age of five, he was formally enthroned as the 14th Dalai Lama and given his new name: Jetsun Jamphel Ngawang Lobsang Yeshe Tenzin Gyatso—Holy Lord, Gentle Glory, Eloquent, Compassionate, Learned Defender of the Faith, and Ocean of Wisdom.

He had to abide by the rules, and you could say he had to develop a "false self," the holy and sovereign leader he would show to the world. Those training him wondered if they had made a mistake about this young man. The truth is, as defined as his *dharma* seemed to be, the Dalai Lama had to choose to follow his *dharma*. It is not simply automatic.

He lived a life of isolation in two palaces, one for summer and one for winter, and every moment was scripted and formalized. Tradition determined how he could talk, walk, and hold his body. His followers were not allowed to look at him, and there was no real conversation other than formality. The Dalai Lama had to gaze above the heads of those speaking to him, as it was sacrilege for him to meet their eyes. The wounding continued. The Gift needs to be reflected, and he was not allowed to see or be seen by the very people whose *dharma* it was for him to lead.

In 1950, when he was only 15 years old, the Chinese invaded Tibet, and the country was ravaged. They looked to the young Dalai Lama to save them. His entire perfect life was thrust into chaos, and he had to flee his country. He was isolated from the people he loved and deeply lonely, not at all educated in the affairs of the world, and this great mantle of responsibility was placed on his young shoulders. He turned to his faith, Buddhism, not because he was the reincarnation of a holy lineage, but because he was afraid, lost, and needed a compass to find a direction for himself and his people. He surrendered to the teachings of his Buddhist faith, to the *dharma,* and by doing so found the reflection of his own greatness. He drew his *dharma* into the very core of his being.

Sometimes all we have is our faith. That is the true power and reason for faith, because there are times on the path to realizing your dharma that scare the wits out of you. There are times when your fate meets your free will, and faith becomes a movement of the heart and mind into a higher dimension of consciousness, because what you have going for you without it isn't enough to deal with the situation. It's as if you tap into a well that others before you who have lived their *dharma* have sourced from, and in so doing, you come back to your own Source. Fortified with his intention to fully embody the sacred teachings of the Buddha, the Dalai Lama became a powerful and compassionate leader for the Tibetan people, working to sustain the hopes and well-being of millions of Tibetan people in exile. He appealed to the United Nations, which led to three resolutions, but his request to China to respect human rights went unheeded. Much bloodshed and destruction followed.

In 1967, at 32 years old, the Dalai Lama embarked on a world tour and met Pope John VI and other world leaders, carrying the pain of his people in his ever-expanding heart; a messenger promoting non-violence and freedom through dialogue and compassion. In 1989, he was awarded the Nobel Peace Prize, and almost anyone alive today over the age of 10 has heard of the Dalai Lama, whose religion is kindness.

His faith helped him stay the course so he could bring his gifts to the world. He holds so much light that it is hard for us to imagine how much darkness his very being metabolizes every day for our planet.

Ambition of the Soul

In the epic journey of our lives, each of us carries a unique frequency on the heart wavelength. It's a privilege to be given the task of announcing that to the world, whether you are a mother or the Dalai Lama. There is room for hesitation, for we are all afraid, but you must stay the course. It is the greatest of all heartaches if you don't.

There is only one of you and your presence changes the world. In fact, everything changed to accommodate the presence of you. The most potent contribution you can make is to be YOU—to fulfill your *dharma*. You are what you do with your uniqueness, and no one else can do that. You will know how to act when you know who you are.

In the *Bhagavad Gita*, Krishna said to Arjuna, "It is better to fail at your own dharma than to succeed at the dharma of someone else." Loving your destiny gives you grace and power. When you are aligned with your destiny, you are aligned with the Infinite. This is the *amor fati* I spoke of earlier. For most of us, if we are honest, there is a core passion that says "I can't not do that." The pain of not doing it would be too big.

To follow your destiny, you must trust and be prepared for the loss of identity required to gain the authentic self. You must connect with the sad/mad/afraid parts of you if your authentic self is to emerge. You must trust in the innate force of human beings to evolve, and you must find that trust within yourself. Destiny is a soul-based directive.

Many spiritual people eschew the ego, and in so doing, fail to make a distinction between the two kinds of ambition and cut themselves off from the yearning of the Soul to make a difference in a big way. Two things are needed to fulfill your *dharma*: ambition and vision.

Your *dharma* has to do with the ambition of your Soul, not your ego. The ambition of the Soul is balanced with humility, which gives it great power. It always addresses the greater good and Spirit becomes your boss. You cannot control your destiny, but you can take charge by handing it over to Spirit. If the Soul takes the lead, ambition follows the Soul, and you live your life differently, seeing success as grace-filled power. If the ego takes the lead, it does not think about the casualties to you or anyone else, as it is driven by fear.

The ambition of the Soul requires a balancing of the masculine and feminine qualities. The feminine is the fuel and the masculine is the direction. The fuel is love and the direction is upward. It is a movement we all come into synch with eventually, in the 5th Dimension. Right now, the downward pull of the 3rd and 4th dimensions is wreaking massive destruction on our planet. All who read this now are called to come out of hiding and use the ambition of the Soul to create positive change.

There is only futile ambition without vision. To stand in your vision you must slow down enough to listen to the pulse of the Universe. Anything short of that is a repetition of the past. When you attune to that living pulse of life, which is the frequency of nature, or in a sense, the earth breathing, you connect with an evolutionary force that moves life forward. Remaining connected to the earth will ground you enough, in most cases, to feel the vibration of your own *dharma*. Being in nature will support you if you are questioning how to offer your *original medicine* to the world. It will help attune you to a global frequency where we are all one, which inspires a person do their great work, despite and often because of heartache.

Forgiveness

There is a vital place for what is traditionally called forgiveness in the realization of one's *dharma*. Forgiveness is for the sake of giveness—we give a kind of blessing to the person who wronged us, releasing them of their debt to us. When we do not release the debt, we keep ourselves linked with the other person in an unhealthy way, which causes us to be held back in other areas of our lives. My not forgiving you or myself is a way of holding myself back from giving again, and to live your *dharma*, you must live full-out.

Wikipedia defines forgiveness as "the intentional and voluntary process by which a victim undergoes a change in feelings and attitude regarding an offense, lets go of negative emotions such as vengefulness, with an increased ability to wish the offender well." I think this is a great definition because forgiveness is intentional, there is transformation, and the vibration of the person forgiving is elevated.

Grief is required for true forgiveness. You must grieve the loss of what was taken from you. That includes feeling and surrendering the emotions that arise, including anger. You surrender all judgment. Let yourself get to *Zero*. It is liberating. You are then free of the need to be somebody other than yourself—an angry and bitter person who seeks justice. In place of dissatisfaction with ourselves, we need to appreciate ourselves and whoever else is involved for doing the best we could. Even a person committing a heinous crime is doing the best they can, given the pain they carry.

Wherever you continue to hold a grievance against another person, you leak energy that could help you fulfill your dharma. The most important person to forgive is yourself if you want to fulfill your dharma. The voice inside your head must transform from judgment to compassion for your fear, struggle, pain, and all you've gone through. Marianne Williamson says, "Forgiveness is not always easy. At times, it feels more painful than the wound we suffered, to forgive the one that inflicted it. And yet, there is no peace without forgiveness."

I have shared some of the wounding I experienced in the relationship with my father, who was both a fierce and fiercely-loving man. He was very responsible and cared for and protected his family with a passion. His sense of humor, storytelling abilities, and big presence endeared him to everyone in our large extended family and beyond. He was called "Red" for his bright red hair and fiery disposition, and he always seemed bigger than his actual size, which was diminished by the limp from childhood polio.

At some point, while deeply involved in my own personal therapy, I was gifted with a vision that took me back to my father's own childhood. He longed to be held by his mother, but she was severely disabled with rheumatoid arthritis and in chronic pain much of the time. When he was old enough, my dad went from pharmacy to pharmacy picking up her "medicine," which was the pain reliever of the day, paregoric—a tincture of opium. I remember her only as a very tiny woman with a big spirit, confined to bed.

The bigger picture of my father's life unfolded before my eyes as he finally found the love of his life, my mother, and then had me. He adored me, and then came my sister. He adored her, and then came my brother. This was within three-and-a-half years, and when the four-year-old Kathleen asked for what was "too much" in his eyes, he was triggered and took it out on me. This particular incident set the stage for much of what unfolded in my life, and my father played his role—a very important role. From a traditional therapeutic perspective, he was my perpetrator, and I was his victim—an abused child. From that moment, the chemistry of my brain and my developing false self (personality) began to shape the contours of my life and

I became a fierce defender of those less strong than I. From the standpoint of spiritual intelligence, this was the wound that cracked me open.

My father played a role that only he could play, and this was my *karma* with him. As I did the work of transformation in therapy, the much larger picture of my father's life and its connection to my life unfolded before me, and the love he had for me was strong enough to reach through the defenses I had built. I connected with my dad on a soul level and felt the grief and remorse that he held as a result of the rupture between us. After years of anger and hurt, I felt only love for him. I was now moving in the direction of my *dharma*. True forgiveness is when you realize that there is nothing to forgive. When I say that I am grateful for my father and all that our turbulent relationship offered me, I mean that from the deepest part of my being.

I am so much like my dad, with the same fiery disposition and red hair, and I would not be writing this book now if it were not for him. Much of the strength, determination, and resilience I claim as gifts were developed as a result of what happened in my childhood. By doing my own work of transformation, I believe I have healed time backwards, and I have taken my dad off the hook for what he did to me. I have completed the *karma* with my father so I could step into my *dharma*. It has taken my entire life.

Forgiveness is an expression of love that allows us to see through new eyes, from the viewpoint of grace. You ask what you need to learn, and you are guided over the mountain of pain as you return to love, which begets love. When the miracle of forgiveness happens, there is a release of endorphins that floods a person with joy and a kind of ambition. A new energy emerges that wants to make things right.

If you need to forgive yourself for all the years or resources you have wasted not being fully who you are, take this moment. In this very moment you could bestow forgiveness upon yourself and release what is in the way. Don't try to figure out why you have been afraid, or have procrastinated, or lost your ambition, or did whatever "dumb" things you have done. Extend forgiveness to yourself by dropping the story you have about yourself. Feel what is really there. It is always some version of fear. Have mercy on the one who feels afraid. Remember, if the voice inside your head causes you distress, it is not the voice of your Soul, but of your ego. Listen for the merciful voice of guidance. It is always there, even if you cannot hear it. That is when faith steps in.

Dharma, devotion, and doubt

You unfold your *dharma* by having great devotion. Devotion at the level of heart bypasses mundane time/space reality. To be devoted, you must know what you are devoted to.

A sign in my office hangs over my chair:

Discipline is Remembering What I Want

It catches people's attention, and we are off-and-running on that question of "What do I really want?" Sometimes people get stuck right there, on the question, but in truth, we all have desires, sometimes hidden from ourselves and often from the world because it would feel like too much pressure to sing the song in your heart out loud. So often we judge it before it ever takes flight.

In order to create something new, we must feel the surge of the current between Here and There that runs through our heart and illumines the possibility of what we want to be born. Deep devotion is what holds you steady all along the way. Devotion is the YES that takes the risk of raising a child, building a business, creating art, or falling in love. Deep devotion has a kind of quiet enthusiasm to it, which comes from the root word *entheos*, literally, *the God within.*

It takes courage to stand up to the saboteur inside who would have us play a smaller game and become cynical rather than devoted. This sub-personality that all humans have to a greater or lesser degree has a vibration of scarcity. It could manifest as an addiction, doubt, hiding, emotional drama, and other defenses against living with our hearts wide open, which is what it means to have courage.

Doubt is a paralyzing affliction—a form of fear that undermines our belief in ourselves and points to the hidden belief in not-enoughness. Doubt is a form of resistance, but remember that beneath the resistance is the love of your *True Self*, your *loveseed*—this kernel of infinity that you are.

Why bother to devote yourself? Because the pain of living in exile from your *True Self* is the deepest kind of pain and is both repetitive and unnecessary. It is based in fear, not love, and therefore, is a diminished way to live. There are so many things you can do to receive the support and find your way, but the desire to do so must be fierce and strong. This is the *Vow* and there is no way around it. You either say yes or you say no. Each time you say YES instead of no to what you are afraid of, you face your fear and liberate yourself from its grasp. The world becomes a much grander place as you step into your own bigness, without apology. Every star in your orbit is given permission to twinkle.

When you say YES to your *dharma*, you are saying YES to effort, freedom, focus, dedication, and co-creation with Spirit. This is an emergent evolutionary process and sometimes we are given the opportunity to make big leaps, to "dare the dark" as Marianne Williamson says. When we do that, we take back the power we lost to fear, which is but the perception of our own mind and gain access to the misty blue planet of the possible.

CHAPTER 12

The Misty Blue Planet of the Possible

"We are but visitors on this planet.
We are here for ninety or one hundred years
at the very most. During that period, we must try to do
something good, something useful with our lives. If you
contribute to other people's happiness, you will find the
true goal, the true meaning of life."
– Dalai Lama

Mastering the movement

In this final chapter, I pick up the threads of deeper understanding around such topics as narcissism, wounding, shame, and the multiplicity of dimensions that are not visible to the human eye, which I have written about in the previous chapters. I will weave the deep colors of these threads with the threads from the thoughts of others who see our present world with fresh eyes and who come from the enlightened knowing that is growing in an ever-widening "tribe" of people worldwide.

This tribe was named the Cultural Creatives by Paul H. Ray and Sherry Anderson, who wrote *The Cultural Creatives: How 50 Million People Are Changing the World.* They were called to dismantle and identify the encodings and the myths that have held us captive. The Creatives are part of a tribe of "Earthkeepers," who were originally the indigenous tribes that shaman and author Alberto Villoldo speaks of when he said, "The visions of the future come as possibilities, because everything in the future is still in potential form. That's why the Earthkeepers from the Hopi, the Maya, the Inka, and many other nations gather regularly to pray for peace on earth. They do so by tracking along the possible futures for the planet to find the one in which the rivers and air are clean, and people live in harmony with nature. The act of finding this desirable future installs it into our collective destiny and makes it a bit more probable than it was before, because it has acquired another quant of energy from these Earthkeepers."

Present-day Earthkeepers hold values that embrace a deep appreciation and care for the world and its ecosystem and all people. They are people whose global heart is awakened and are called to serve in some way. They are involved in self-actualization through psychotherapy, shamanism, spiritual practice, and forms of activism for peace and social justice. You are most likely one of them if you have read this far, or are possibly experiencing an awakening, which is my intention.

Now that you have the various pieces of the *Path of Zero*, I want to bring it all together for you, because it is the path that returns you to your innocence, which is at the leading edge of thought and creation. The *Path of Zero* establishes a bridge that you can cross to your enlightened innocence, which is infused with vitality, strength, hope, compassion, and resolve. Tap on the center of your chest now as you read these words to activate that inspired energy: *I am open to seeing new possibilities. I am connected to the Source of all power.*

I will describe the *Path of Zero* in seven distinct steps that allow your linear mind to relax and gather focus. We need that part of us at times, in balance with our imaginal and intuitive selves. You will notice that I did not market this book as a seven-step method to reach enlightenment or joy or abundance. I don't "believe" in steps for the sake of steps. They seem to require that so much of the linear and analytical brain be online that the emotional body is left lagging—a kind of soul lag. With soul lag, you aren't ever fully present to your life. You can go through the motions without ever being there. These "steps" are part of a natural flow of experience you can respond to from the most conscious part of yourself—your highest self.

What I have discovered in my personal work and with many others is that there are key elements you must master to become an intentional co-creator on planet Earth; someone who can make a difference and live outside the restrictions of the encodings that infect us all from growing up in a corrupt and extremely limited system. To live as a person who embodies values beyond the common cultural attitude that "shit happens" (that saying triggers me so much I had to write a book!) means that you must take the time to learn, reflect, ask, research, and question the heck out of "authority" and all belief systems that contract your consciousness, rather than expand it. Only the latter is in synch with the Universe.

In this chapter I will weave in, out and around the seven steps both as review and to give the process an even larger context. Here are the steps:

1. Set your highest intention.
2. Witness without judgment.
3. Feel what you feel.
4. Examine the story.
5. Surrender to *Zero*.
6. Accept everything.
7. Receive the gift.

Remember, because you are both wave and particle, a powerful energy field begins to surround you when you take this path, as you learn to cross that bridge back and forth between your human and Divine self. This is the movement of creation. As you do that over and over, you begin to bring those you love with you, which can strengthen your resolve to become masterful in this movement.

The mother of all myths

In discovering Paul Levy's penetrating teaching on how to break the spell of evil, I found a kindred spirit. Levy shows us that within the very force that can destroy us lies the hope of what can save our world at this time. In his book *Dispelling Wetiko*, Levy describes *wetiko* as a non-local, transcendental force that cannot be adequately expressed in language, because it is not a thing. Think of *wetiko* as the *downward pull* in virtual virus form on steroids.

Wetiko is an Algonquian Indian word describing a mercurial and elusive psychic phenomenon that has both material and spiritual aspects. Native American cosmology is similar to Eastern traditions in that the Universe is regarded as a dream of the Creator and is a dream in which all the characters in the dream are dreaming as well. In such a cosmology, *wetiko* is often depicted as cannibalistic spirits that embody the worst qualities of human nature and which can take possession of a human being. Once human, *wetikos* are considered to have lost their minds and exist as crazy, wild creatures that no longer live according to acceptable limits, engaging in excesses of every kind.

The *wetiko* virus is passed down trans-generationally, over multiple generations. Unlike other psychiatric disorders such as schizophrenia, bipolar disorder, depression, ADHD, and the countless anxiety disorders that are rampant, the *wetiko* psycho-pathogen cannot be controlled with medication, because the medication would come from the very system that is infected with the virus. Overuse of Big Pharma medication is contributing to people being more susceptible to the *wetiko* virus, which thrives in a climate void of authentic feeling. Overuse of technology invites *wetiko* to inhabit your psyche.

This rampant and seemingly unlimited capacity for self-deception that afflicts humanity at this point is like a pact with the devil. Essentially, this is the *false self* on steroids, and all our systems of government are infected with the *wetiko* virus and thus, all our leaders.

According to Levy—and I concur—though *wetiko* has no intrinsic power, it is a "virtual reality" that has enough energy to attack and destroy all of humanity when we collude with the ancient myth—the mother of all myths—that we are separate. Imagine that power! We get separated and cut off due to trauma—cut off from our innocence, from our *loveseeds.* Then we feed off ourselves and everyone else, and the virus of *wetiko* takes over. And it is all built on a lie. What if we could reclaim and harness that power?

What Levy calls *wetikos* are the countless human beings who suffer from not being able to feel, and who have no desire to change that, thus cutting themselves off from their own energy source. What's more, without being able to feel, they must draw energy from outside sources, at times behaving as energy vampires. Those who are infected are at risk of being completely overtaken by this virus, thus causing them to take a perverse pleasure in the ability to dominate and inflict brutality on others, out of a primitive instinct to be the most powerful.

If that sounds like sociopathology and possibly psychopathology, you are not far off base. It's just that it is so rampant, and no DSM diagnosis begins to adequately describe the power and nature of *wetiko.* It is even affecting the mental health profession in a profound way, which has become infected by insurance companies and the present medical system, all corrupted by Big Pharma and the Corporations who make millions as more people are infected by the *wetiko* virus. By shining the light of awareness on what is happening, we can call it what it is—a virus that is affecting everyone all the time.

But Levy warns us that though *wetiko* comes from us, it is not simply "all in the mind" and therefore "not real." You may deny it or ignore it, but doing so will not prevent you from being affected by it, any more than we could be safe in saying that because we don't believe in malaria, we are immune to its ravages should we be bitten by an infected mosquito.

We need to look at this stuff. There is no way to bypass it, because there has been and continues to be so much trauma. After the San Bernardino terrorist shooting by a couple in December 2015, I faced my own *wetiko* as I was walking down the main street of the happy little village I lived in. I saw the woman from the couple over and over on television, always in a burka. A few days after the shooting, I encountered a woman in a burka walking toward me and found myself immediately filled with rage, about to sneer. I saw what I imagined was an uneasy look on the woman's face. I was so familiar with witnessing myself that I caught it "in a heartbeat" and quickly let it go. I got to *Zero* fast. I smiled, and she smiled back, and I felt a real connection. I sensed that she did, as well.

We don't need to look to terrorists to see full-blown *wetikos*, as the major political parties at this very moment are hosting the virus. It is not the politicians that are the problem, though you would think so if you believed the mainstream media. Understand that the real problem is how many people are affected by the *wetiko* virus in order for Big *Wetikos* to rise up the way they have. Crowds get riled up, and while they seem emotional, they are feeling the rage that covers up terror, and rage and terror are two primal instincts from the lower brain. Feeling involves the heart, and an open one at that—a kind of innocence that is stronger than 10,000 shields, and more powerful than the *wetiko* virus could ever be.

Emergent noetics arising out of ancient wisdom

In truth, our modern world is making its own descent—one in which we are all participating, whether consciously or not. The world is enmeshed in dreams within dreams. Governments, religions, systems of law, financial systems, and traditional healing and educational modalities are all stricken with the *wetiko* virus. Our fundamental rules of relating to one another are breaking down, and massive chaos is unfolding.

How do we reconcile our need to do something about the suffering with these thoughts by the present-day spiritual teacher, Adyashanti? In *Emptiness Dancing* he writes, "True sacred relationship with this moment flowers when we are not asking it to be anything other than it is. Then the beauty blossoms. But if we ask the smallest thing of this moment, we start to miss the beauty. Our asking distorts what we are able to see and experience in ourselves."

Most spiritual teachers and channels reconfirm the imminence of humanity's awakening, and yet many of you keep allowing yourselves to be drawn back into doubt by the *wetiko* manifested everywhere as suffering and corruption. Some of you feel intuitively called to physically assist in alleviating it by working with charities or by going to areas where you can personally help. But if you cannot or are not drawn to do so, don't dwell on the suffering. Instead, send love, compassion, and healing to any areas that particularly concern you, or even to the whole world. Feel what reverberates within you and surrender those feelings and thoughts, dropping them into the Sacred Heart. Know that your powerfully-held intentions are extremely effective, and rejoice when you can, knowing all is well.

Thinking that they don't want to "feed the darkness," many people turn away from the suffering of the world and thus their own darkness. True, we don't want to feed it, but true peace emanates from inside our own *loveseed*, and the only way to reach it is through the darkness. The world of flesh and blood and the hell or heaven in our minds and hearts interpenetrate each other, and we are the conduits through which the energy flows.

We fall under the spell of our own narcissistic self-absorption when we consistently avoid the world "out there." By dissociating ourselves from the larger world, we avoid engaging with parts of ourselves and unwittingly donate to the cause of *wetiko*. You may not be called to action, but you can be proactive in your conscious embodiment of the presence of your being and profoundly affect the larger field of existence. Combine this with inspired action, and you amp up the light in the field.

My friend Gary Stamper says in *Awakening the New Masculine*, "Most activists are addicted to doing, and many spiritual people are just as addicted to being. Sacred Activism is a transforming force of do-be-do-be-do—compassion in action that is born of a fusion of deep spiritual knowledge, courage, love and passion with wise radical action in the world."

Whether actual activists or carriers of the activist archetype, political activists often fight against evil in the system as if it is outside of themselves. In doing so they feed the very thing they are fighting. They perpetrate the aggression that creates the polarization that Levy calls "the calling card of *wetiko*" in his book *Dispelling Wetiko*.

Spiritual people of every ilk, from the fundamentalist Rapturists who believe they will be taken off planet Earth by Jesus Christ to the fundamentalists of the New Age movement who disavow all things dark, fail to use their imaginal capacity and interpret spiritual teachings literally, rather than understanding them metaphorically. Yes, we are already perfect and enlightened in the absolute sense, but in the nuts and bolts of 3rd dimensional existence, we may be far from enlightened in our treatment of ourselves, the people in our lives, and the Earth. Misuse of the high metaphysical teachings is a form of *wetiko*, all based on the myth of separation.

While living in Peru, I learned from Andean paqos (Inca shamans) about the darker energies and how they come in through the *qusqu* or third chakra, which is the power chakra. In Andean medicine, *hoocha* refers to dark or dense energy inside and outside of ourselves. It is the Andean version of *wetiko*, or what we would call evil. The gut is a sensitive area of the body that is vulnerable to having powerful energies intrude, which can manifest as illness in the digestive system or in the area of the lower back or reproductive organs. A vast majority of people today are afflicted with *hoocha*, and they are not getting well with modern medicine.

Andean medicine is based on our connection with Pachamama, which is the Earth, and the Apus, which are the mountains reaching to heaven. By making this deep connection with the earth and filling ourselves with light that we raise up through our bodies and energy field, we can transform and release the *hoocha* that we may be holding in our energy bodies. They believe that this is how we can protect ourselves. It is the light that protects us from the darkness and the raising of the vibration within the body and energy field. Without the light, we are totally vulnerable to the downward pull.

We need to recognize that we can take on *hoocha* from the outside world and that we often generate *hoocha* in ourselves and project it outward onto others and onto the world, strengthening the illusion of separateness. Most often *hoocha* is the result of a need for power that is compensation for not feeling good enough or of fear of abandonment or being hurt again. In other words, *hoocha* is the result of unhealed wounds.

The Andean solution to this is *ayni,* or reciprocity. The experience of *ayni* dissolves the illusion of separateness and mitigates any sense of scarcity that can lead to feeling powerless. Some of the great modern thinkers like Ken Wilber speak about this ancient wisdom as "we-space" to describe spaces in which we let go of seeing from the "I" and transcend the limitations of seeing from that perspective. The top down style of "I" thinking has brought us to this grand imbalance in every area of existence. There is a shift in emergent thinking that engages in problem solving using group intelligence.

What we need are we-spaces in which each person in the collective has done the work of dealing with his or her own *hoocha,* from their personal power shadow. At this time, humanity needs we-spaces in which there are practices and structures that support communion, so that each "I" sees the other "I" as pure Spirit reflected. To evoke this in shared space can be powerful medicine and must be driven by love itself.

It is possible that, as the Buddhist teacher Thich Nhat Hanh says in the Inquiring Mind article entitled "The Next Buddha May Be a Sangha": "The next Buddha will not take the form of an individual, but rather of a community practicing understanding and loving kindness, a community practicing mindful living. And the practice can be carried out as a group, as a city, as a nation."

Holy unrest

Do you feel the holy unrest? It is part of the human condition, arising out of the tension of opposites—most profoundly, the tension between our human and divine natures. This freedom to choose poses a great dilemma, and we must not be blinded by the symptoms of unrest that arise from the ancient fear, but rather, we must walk through them.

If you pay homage to the god of indifference, it doesn't mean you are exempt from the changes being asked of you. The descent of humanity is needed in order to shake up these beliefs and to release the illusions that go with them. **Being alive today means you are Witness to the death of an old paradigm of separateness and protection and the birth of an emerging paradigm of connection and sharing.** You are either holding onto the old for dear life or opening to the new.

In truth, that which represents the biggest fear in you is the thing you must face in order to dissolve the old reality and the story you made up about what to be afraid of. There is a gridwork or matrix inside your physical body and within the larger field that holds these old realities in place. Every time you release the fear-based feelings, you collapse the gridwork. You keep the limits of the gridwork in place when you hold onto old fears or shut down.

Those limits are your limits, and they are inside your physical body and you are within the larger gridwork, for as within, so without. It all has to go. There truly is a physical dimension waiting for you that does not hold those old limits anymore. Your physical body is trying to walk in an unlimited dimension and cannot bring the old programs and beliefs and energy with it, for they are too dense. It is important to pay attention to where you are allowing yourself to be "stuck" in an old, limiting reality.

What really helps is creative expression through movement, art, writing, poetry, music, and the countless other ways creativity longs to express itself. The creative part of us lives outside the matrix or gridwork, which is the same as the "dream" in indigenous cultures, where people are sleepwalking. The creative spark in us remains untouched by the influences from parents and culture, and, in fact, the more we go against the grain of the "norm," the deeper and richer the creative part of us becomes. The artistic impulse is the impulse to create and evolve and reach beyond. By connecting with this impulse, an artist can express the deepest longings of the collective. American bass singer and activist Paul Leroy Robeson said, "Artists are the gatekeepers of truth. We are civilization's radical truth."

In truth, we are all artists sculpting our lives either from our regrets or our dreams; our fears or our deep love; our shoulds or our felt desires. Each time we say YES to our felt desire, we harness the power of love, for desire is from our essence, our loveseed, which is the strongest force in the Universe. As American playwright Tennessee Williams said in *The Follies of God*, "We are saved only by love—love for each other and the love that we pour into the art we feel compelled to make."

Some people believe we have been preplanned for enslavement by off-planet beings. Honestly, I don't know if it's true that humanity is being "dumbed down" through tampering with our food system, among other things. It doesn't matter because it is all *wetiko*, and shifting that is up to us. The entire history of humanity is rooted in fear, and we must loop back and question where we have come from and where we are going, question our outdated ways and clear out the fear to make room for new depths.

Collapsing the gridwork

Let's look at a few ways we can collapse the gridwork now, without having to fight aliens. Look at the "justice" system. Presently, we have a system that says you are unworthy until you prove otherwise, especially to black men. In Richmond, California, the Office of Neighborhood Safety created a Peacemaker Fellowship. In their city alone, they discovered that 70% of crime was being done by 28% of the population. They addressed this 28% and helped them. They've had a 79% success rate, 73% fewer homicides, and 71% fewer firearm assaults.

That is one city, and it is great action because it deals with what the people needed, rather than beliefs. So many of the programs for racial justice simply don't work because the entire system is based upon the lie that there is actually a separate Negroid race. Fighting racism within a system that believes in the lie of race is pure *wetiko*.

Beliefs can tie us up in knots and strip us of our humanity and our innocence. We were all human before

we had a belief. When you have beliefs, you can let them go, but when they have you, it's hard to escape. We ingest beliefs from parents, siblings, school, songs, and so on. When they crystallize and fuse together, we form an identity around them.

Another insidious belief is that we are separate from nature. When the first chakra is disconnected from the feminine Earth, we can feel orphaned and motherless. The masculine principle takes over and we look for security from material things. Individuality prevails over interconnectedness, and selfish drives trump social and global responsibility. The more separated we become from the Earth, the more alien we become to the feminine, causing us to disown our passions, creativity and sexuality. Through the grapevine I heard a medicine woman from the Amazon say that the real reason the rain forest is being cut down is because it is wet and dark and tangled and feminine. Let that sink in. We live on a sexual planet, and we are part of her.

The main challenge for each of us is the quest to enlarge the soul and liberate the spirit. I call this personal alchemy, and it is the art of transforming the base aspects of our human selves into the glorious gold of our Higher Selves. All the rest of our problems are made up! It's not about religion, race, ideologies, nations, or any of what the daily news is saturated with. Politics will always fail us, as the true revolution is within. Religion is an attempt to nail down the infinite. It is about reduction rather than expansion and goes against the natural flow of the Universe.

No guru can do the work for you. Each person must go through the personal ordeal or initiation of self-transformation, which at times involves a complete dismantling of perception and beliefs, and which involves receiving the gift, which is the final step of the *Path of Zero*. The gift you take away from your own transformation is what contributes to seeding the higher dimensions that are beyond the beliefs and machinations of *wetiko*.

One of the beliefs we must urgently question is the belief in security, which is often tied to money. The truth is, there is enough for everyone. It's simply not distributed in the most loving way, and striving for personal security is part of the problem. The Sufficiency Movement is devoted to transforming the illusion of scarcity into a deep and sustainable commitment to the principle of sufficiency. Sufficiency is not an amount, but is rather a way of being, seeing, and living. In *The Soul of Money*, author Lynne Twist wisely states, "When you let go of trying to get more of what you don't really need, it frees up oceans of energy to make a difference with what you already have."

To embrace sufficiency is a radical step that could very well transform the planetary understanding of economics and wealth. The old economic structure does not work for the majority of people who want to live their truth, many of whom are artists and healers who have something important to offer. It is still an inside job, however, and the fact that the government does not support art may be a greater gift than many starving artists and healers realize. You don't want your creativity to be regulated!

The fear of not having enough money causes you to emanate a vibration that prevents you from receiving what you want. For me, the feeling I receive from having financial wealth is freedom, so I focus on the freedom, and when I do, I always have more than enough. The spiritual name given to me in India is *Aditi*, which means "boundless, entire," or "freedom, security" in Sanskrit. Part of my own *Hero's Journey* has been to live into the vibration of that name.

When you begin to see that genuine wealth is really well-being, and that the real meaning of prosperity is to feel whole and hopeful and full of possibility, you are well on your way to transforming your relationship with money.

Builders of the future

A decade ago, a young woman named Maggie Doyne wasn't really sure what she wanted to do with her life, and she knew she wasn't ready for college. At 18, she knew she wanted to make a difference, and she liked to travel, so she took a gap year and combined the two. She ended up in Nepal, where she "fell in love with the country and the people." She was amazed that even though they had so little, and though over one million children had been orphaned or abandoned during the horrific years of being taken over by the Chinese, the people were gracious, and they still had hope.

Maggie met a young girl named Hima, whom she saw every day on the side of the dry riverbed, hauling rocks and hammering them into little pieces that she sold for a dollar. She was helping to feed and house her family. Every day Maggie saw Hima who would bow, saying "Namaste," which is Sanskrit for "I bow to the divine within you." When Maggie asked her guide why Hima wasn't in school, she discovered that there were no schools. In that Satori moment, she vowed that someday there would be no more children in the riverbed, and 10 years later that is true. Spending $5,000 in savings from her babysitting days, Maggie bought land and worked with the community to build a school, a women's center, and the Kopila Valley Children's Home. Her BlinkNow Foundation now supports these efforts. Their motto is "In the blink of an eye, we can all make a difference."

As she received the 2015 CNN Hero of the Year award, Maggie said, "If you had told me when I turned 18 that I was going to be the mom of 50 kids, I would have told you that you were totally crazy. And I am. And to my kids, I love you so much. Don't ever forget how much I love you. And to the country of Nepal, thank you so much for loving me and accepting me as a daughter welcoming me into your country. And to all of you in this room and who are watching, please, please remember that we have the power to create the world that we want to live in, just as we want it."

I have always thought that rather than ambitiously striving straight on to college, it makes far more sense for high school graduates to spend at least two years doing some form of service for which they receive a stipend to live, whether it be abroad or here in the States. There is so much needed in every possible way, and the experience would enrich every person in ways untold.

Envision this: hundreds of thousands of *angels of love*—young Americans of every kind, every ethnic background, every socioeconomic class, every level of education, every sexual orientation—just out of high school, about to enter the world. We support them to serve as an army of love and goodwill, and they forego the conditioned response to get married, have kids, and get divorced in total disillusionment. They see what needs to be done and simply do it, on their own terms, with our blessing and support. And they care very much.

This model is used by many Christian Church organizations, where young members go on "mission." It would require a fundamental shift in perception (a miracle of great magnitude) for the average conditioned American, colonized by our affluent and success-driven culture, to shake off the *wetiko* of the present model. That is one of the reasons I have written this book—so you can begin to see with the eyes of the heart and think with the soul of a master, sourced from your *loveseed*.

In addition to busting the myth that you must go to college, Maggie's story busts the myth that you need to set a goal to have a powerful outcome. Rather, you need to take a courageous step toward what you really want so you can get into the flow, and life can lead you in the direction your soul has been going all along. It's much bigger than any one goal or decision. It is about pure intention, which you come to once you pass through the resistance to it.

The possible

We have almost come full circle now. Let's stop for a moment and reflect on the journey we have taken together, toward the possibility of a world that is truly at peace. I promised you some miracles, which you now know is a shift in perception. You also know that there is only one Sacred Heart and that the entire Universe is contained within it.

I heard the story of Craig Sager, a very colorful sportscaster who is ill with leukemia and yet continues to be a bright light in his message. He said something so profound, particularly as he is nearing the end of his life: "Time is something that can't be bought. Time is simply how you live your life."

Ending this book with one of my favorite stories is the gift I want to give you now. Many of you have heard it, but a good story never dies. Like time, it's something that cannot be bought and is relevant to how you live your life.

Called *The Rabbi's Gift,* by Dr. M. Scott Peck in his book *The Different Drum*, the actual author is unknown. Each time I hear it, I find myself vibrating several octaves higher, and it is *this* feeling we will come to know more intimately in the new world we are co-creating. The story goes like this:

There was once monastery that fell upon hard times, and lost the beauty and grandeur it once was. The Order was well-known across the land, but due to waves of anti-monastic persecution, the monastery was decimated to almost nothing. In the decaying mother house, only five monks were left and all were over 70. The Order and its members were literally dying.

Deep woods surrounded the monastery, which included a hermitage often used by a local rabbi. Due to years of prayer and contemplation, the old monks were very intuitive, and one or the other always sensed when the rabbi was in his hermitage. "The rabbi is in the woods. The rabbi is in the woods again," they whispered to each other.

The abbot of this monastery was deeply-troubled about his dying Order, and decided to visit the rabbi to seek his wisdom, as a last chance to come up with a plan to save his beloved monastery.

Having known of each other for years, the rabbi welcomed the abbot into his hut in the woods. When the rabbi heard of the sad dilemma, he commiserated with the abbot, saying that he indeed knew how it is, and even shared that the spirit had gone out of the people in his own town, which is why he came to the woods to pray. "Almost no one comes to the synagogue anymore," lamented the rabbi.

The two holy men wept together, then read parts of the Torah and spoke of profound things. As the abbot was leaving, they embraced, each declaring that it was wonderful to meet after all these years. The abbot said he felt much better, but his purpose for coming had not been solved, and this weighed upon his heart. "Is there nothing you can tell me? Is there no piece of advice you can give me that would help me save my dying order?"

"I am so sorry my friend. I have no advice, but I do know one thing: the Messiah is one of you."

The other monks eagerly awaited the abbot's return to learn what the wise rabbi had told him. They were saddened to hear that the rabbi had no advice to give, and that the two men had wept and read the Torah. "Was there nothing you learned, Abbot?" The abbot thought a moment, and said, "As I was leaving, he said something mysterious—that the Messiah is one of us."

In the days, weeks and months that followed, this mysterious statement led the old monks to ponder *The Messiah is one of us?* They began to wonder which monk was the Messiah, and to think deeply of the possibility. Could he mean the abbot? Surely it was Father Abbot as he has led our Order for years. But on the other hand, it could be Brother Thomas, who everyone knew as a holy man. When thinking of Brother Eldred, known for his crotchety nature, they doubted he could be the Messiah, but then remembered that he is virtually always right. Surely it could not be Brother Phillip who is so passive and never speaks up. Then again, Phillip has a way of always showing up like an angel when you need him. Maybe Brother Phillip is the Messiah.

Could it be me? thought each of the monks, which both frightened and uplifted them. *What if I am the Messiah?*

Contemplating these things, the old monks began to treat each other with great kindness and extraordinary respect, since there was a chance that any of them might be the Messiah. At that thought, they also began to treat themselves with extraordinary respect and kindness.

The forest surrounding the monastery was so beautiful that people still occasionally came to visit and picnic on its tiny lawn, before wandering along its paths that led to the forest. Now and then others would go into the dilapidated chapel to meditate, and over time, they began to notice a very different feeling in the air. They sensed an aura of extraordinary respect and kindness in the five old monks, who seemed to radiate light and a feeling of peace. This was powerfully attractive to the weary visitors, and hardly knowing why, they returned to the monastery more often to picnic, to play, and to pray. More and more people came, and each person brought friends to share this special place.

And so it happened that some of the younger men who came to visit the monastery sat on the grass and had conversations with the old monks. Some of the young men were called to join the Order, and within a few years, the monastery was once again a thriving Order, known as a vibrant center of light and spirituality that helped bring hope to all the realm. All this, thanks to the rabbi's gift!

Love has an infinite spectrum, and if you wish for the full spectrum of love to be expressed through your humanness, then you must embrace everything about yourself, and everything, including the great miseries and mysteries of the world. To heal the great divide, you must recognize your own divinity in all beings, especially those you want to push away. From this deep acceptance will come visions of the possible.

This is transcendence, and it quickens consciousness and opens the way for miracles. Life on planet Earth is about quality not quantity—about love of family and community, not abstract goals of success. As you simplify your life by continuously taking the *Path of Zero*, you will find that connection is what makes your heart sing, for it is what allows your very *loveseed* to thrive.

It is time to let go of martyrdom and the myth of unworthiness. If you have yet to make a clean break of a bad situation, a relationship, or a job that is just not working for you, set your intention and take action now. It is time to ride the great wave of transformation by becoming one with it rather than being knocked over by it. In any moment, you can choose love and stand up and show your soul. Over time you will become fully lit and other struggling souls will catch your light.

We are birthing a new culture that thrives on kindness and the ability to see the Real in one another. It's a culture that is grounded in the initiation of the wounded healer archetype, and from all the wisdom that has been learned from straying so far from the center of who we are, and transforming to return to our original innocent template.

Our conscious suffering allows us to be stewards of the new worlds wanting to be born in others, including nations that are still confined by old-world limits. Everything becomes global—an awareness from birth of our oneness, and which we teach the children. We want to raise children who are at home in the world, with many varied attachments and sources of nurturance, rather than the nuclear family alone. As consciousness expands, so does our sense of being a global family. Alienation becomes a thing of the past, as more of us embrace our essential connection.

Loveseed is in a dimension all its own, at the heart of all the others. *Loveseed* is the template for a new world.

A Note to Colleagues
(Psychotherapists and Other Healers)

I wrote this book with my fellow psychotherapists and fellow healers in mind, because I know what it means to make healing your *dharma*. In order to continue to do our work, we must continue to experience joy and aliveness as we do it. This is the evolutionary impulse at its best, and I personally know the challenge you must meet to respond to this calling.

There is so much need, so much heartache. It could dampen anyone's spirits to deal with that much pain.

So I wrote this book to remind you of who you are, as I have had to do the same for myself. And I wrote it in such a way that you can give it to the people you serve, with the intention that they expand their minds and hearts beyond their symptoms to the place where true healing takes place. My hope is that they become more open to the *medicine* that you have to offer.

I have always taken comfort in this quote by the Indian guru of non-dualism, Nisargadatta Maharaj: "The mind creates the abyss, the heart crosses it."

So many times I have sat before a person or a couple and not known what to do or say. At some point, after all the meditation retreats, I learned to become so quiet inside and drop my awareness into my heart and even farther down, into my belly, and rest in the not knowing. I learned to breathe up and down and expand, and center in my heart between my belly and my mind, and always something would arise in that space—something new that I trusted could be useful for the person or couple.

I didn't know at the time that this little "trick" I did to alleviate the stress of not knowing was part of my *medicine*—part of how I am able to walk to the edge and be open to something new emerging. I now know the science behind it, but the actual practice was inspired by the concept of being a "hollow bone" that I learned in a psychodrama training in Black Earth, Wisconsin, in 1994, with psychologist and dear friend, Kate Hudgins and a wise Native American teacher named Tahnahga Yako. Becoming a *hollow bone* is an ancient practice in Zen Buddhism, shamanism, and many indigenous healing traditions. It is an inner state of freedom that we can cultivate and requires that we continuously do our own work of clearing the way. I am writing this now to remind you of a few things that I believe can help you keep your vibration high and your mind and heart clear about the privilege we have in being called to do the work we do.

We must consciously realize that we are being asked to be conduits for light to descend and help transform the denser thoughts, emotions, and beliefs that hold people

back. That means we must work at our own edge and continuously be aware of our own darkness.

We need to let go of hiding behind the all-knowing therapist-healer cloak. We can't really address what we cannot see, so we must look below the surface of symptoms in order to help our clients get to the root of their struggles. We cannot do that from behind the wizard's curtain.

That means we must develop new capacities for subtle perception so that we can see possibilities where there were none before. There is an essential level of creation where genuine transformation can occur. It is an edge where what emerges can heal the past because something truly new has been born.

Present-day spiritual teacher Thomas Hübl says, "Healing means that we dedicate our life to where the light meets the shadow. Where aliveness meets the contraction. Where the potential meets the past. Working on that edge is a constant revelation and expansion."

That edge is between you and the person you are working with, and what you bring to that edge is of great importance—it is your *medicine*. You must keep faith in the process, including the difficulties, and keep compassion strong. Let go of fighting with your failings. Most of our suffering is the result of not believing in ourselves, and it takes away from what we are here to do.

We all have *medicine* that comes from our soul. It comes through the wisdom in our message, which is what we have learned on our journey. You being you is what will support your clients to transform and heal. Believe in your own *medicine*.

We must remember that psychotherapy and healing in this new age is always a partnership of body, mind, and spirit. When someone walks into your office, an entire world walks in with them, and we must remember to see people within the larger context of their lives.

I recall the work of therapist Salvador Minuchin, who developed structural family therapy. In the 1960s, while he was Director at Philadelphia Child Guidance Center, research was provided by Children's Hospital of Philadelphia on diabetic children who had a very high number of hospitalizations for acidosis, which is a stress-related condition. These children were not improving with traditional forms of therapy and, based on his work with the psychodynamics of enmeshed families, Minuchin's experiments provided some startling results.

The child was put in a room far away from the parents in an entirely different part of the hospital and the acidosis level was taken. As the parents began to discuss matters and conflict arose between them and time after time the child's acidosis levels began to climb. As family therapist Carl Whitaker said, "There is no such thing as an individual, there are only fragments of families."

Remember, we are entrusted to help each person touch what is true in themselves. If we already decide who they are, that cannot happen. Ditch what you think about "normal" so that you can see the magnificent being in front of you.

In 2010, when I was closing my practice in Northern Virginia, I faced the task of referring my clients to colleagues

I knew could meet them at their healing edge. I was working with a marvelous lesbian couple who were very devoted to their awakening and to co-creating the best relationship they could. They were involved in unconventional sexual practices called *kink* and had all the usual struggles that other couples have around autonomy, surrender, trust, and so on. The subject matter was at times different than with non-*kink* couples, but the struggles were the same.

I reached out to colleagues in an organization I'd been in for years and who were all couples therapists. I explained the situation and asked if anyone would be willing to receive my referral.

Silence. Nada. And then came this email:

> Dear Kathleen,
>
> I would be willing to work with your couple, but only if they are willing to explore their pathology, which I am sure is around some kind of trauma. I don't agree with their lifestyle, because it is simply not normal, but I will work with them if they look at their pathology.

It took all I had not to respond to my "normal" colleague. Scottish psychiatrist R. D. Laing, says it best in *The Politics of Experience and the Bird of Paradise*: "What we call 'normal' is a product of repression, denial, splitting, projection, introjection and other forms of destructive action on experience. It is radically estranged from the structure of being."

Drop your judgments and do not put too much weight on a DSM diagnosis, forgetting to see the magnificent struggle between the divine and human natures in the people you serve.

Remain hopeful, even in the darkest of times. We must become masters of the reframe, offered at the right moment, always holding the tension of the opposites, even when our clients cannot see the light.

They come to us with the wish to alleviate their pain. We must offer them a new way to see their pain, as well. When I asked Eli, the acupuncturist, if he thought I had rheumatoid arthritis and he responded by saying, "You still have a choice," a miracle occurred, and that shift in perception is what allowed me to make choices with the hope of healing.

Remember that in all things there is contained its opposite; that breath and awareness can transform sadness to love, anger to power, and anxiety to excitement and enthusiasm. And as for hope, the Czech writer and statesman Vaclav Havel offers us this perspective: "Hope is definitely not the same thing as optimism. It is not the conviction that something will turn out well, but the certainty that something makes sense, regardless of how it turns out."

The last and most important thing I want to say is to go for the love. Every symptom and every suffering is a doorway back to the original love inside the person—to their loveseed.

If you want to call that love forth in the person, find it within yourself. Find all the ways that the people you work with are like you and attune to that. Get some limbic resonance going. Feel the love. The ones who drive you a bit mad are the greatest teachers, showing you the parts of you that you still refuse to embrace.

I developed such a fondness for the "crabbiest" (her own word) woman I had ever worked with. She would barge into my office, blow out the candle I had been burning all day, open the sliding glass doors, and sit down to say, "That green you are wearing is disgusting." The funny thing is, she was right about that particular green.

She had not come for me to help her with her crabbiness, but to help her with the pain that caused it, and yet somehow, the crabbiness lessened over the years. What I most recall now are the moments she would smile and we would share some delight over an idea, or just the fact that we were sharing the moment. Since she had never felt that with anyone because of her crabbiness, there was "magic" in those moments. I feel only tenderness and gratitude when I think of her.

Go for *those* moments, dear colleagues. Become a "hollow bone" to channel what you came to give. I wrote this book with you in mind. You are the modern-day shamans and medicine men and women of a very stressed-out tribe. Your work is to be conduits of love, for it is only love that heals.

Please pass this book on to the people you serve so that they can begin to see with new eyes. I hope that it makes the work you do richer and more joyful.

With deep love,
Kathleen

About the Author

Kathleen Hanagan is a psychotherapist, modern mystic, and ordained shamanic priestess, whose work integrates the essential wisdom of the great spiritual traditions with scientific knowledge, thirty years working intimately with individuals, couples, and groups, and her own quest for liberation.

With the clarity that comes from one familiar with the territory of the heart, Kathleen shows us how to expand our awareness beyond the subconscious limitations of a culture that has lost its Soul. She teaches us how to remain awake at every stage of the journey, so that we can do what we came to earth to do: to live wholehearted and prosperous lives of loving kindness, generosity and truth.

Her book, ***Loveseed: The Template for Birthing A New World***, shows us how to create miracles through shifts in our perception, that allow us to trance-end the fear that creates personal and collective pain.

To learn more about Kathleen and her work, visit KathleenHanagan.com